ϟϟ REGALIA

SS REGALIA

ROBIN LUMSDEN

With photographs from the collection of
Ulric of England

CHARTWELL
BOOKS, INC.

Published by
BOOK SALES, INC.
114 Northfield Avenue
Raritan Center
Edison, N.J. 08818

Produced by
Brompton Books Corp.
15 Sherwood Place
Greenwich, CT 06830

ISBN 07858-0228-2

Printed in China

PAGE 1: SS troops off-duty.

PAGE 2: SS troops parade at Nuremburg, 1933

PAGE 3: Insignia for an SS-Obersturmführer in SS-LAH.

PAGE 4-5: Fanfare trumpeters of the Leibstandarte-SS 'Adolf Hitler', 1933.

CONTENTS

Origins of the SS   6

The Allgemeine-SS   20

The Waffen-SS   64

The Germanic-SS   144

Index and Acknowledgments   158

ORIGINS OF THE SS

After the defeat of Germany at the end of World War I in November 1918, the government collapsed, revolution swept the country and politics became a dangerous business, with all sides employing strong-arm tactics. Nationalist groups sprang up all over Germany, with the aim of ridding the land of the 'November Traitors' who had brought the disgrace of the dictated peace, and of the Communists and Spartakists whose first loyalty was to Bolshevik Russia. Nationalists came from every level of society, and at the lower end of the Munich social scale was Anton Drexler's tiny German Workers' Party, one of whose meetings Adolf Hitler attended as a military observer in September 1919. He subsequently joined the party and, through his powers of oratory, virtually took it over from the outset, changing its name to the National Socialist German Workers' Party (Nationalsozialistische Deutsche Arbeiterpartei, or NSDAP).

The stewards for the founding meeting of the NSDAP on 24 February 1920 were a squad of *Zeitfreiwilligen*, or temporary volunteers, armed with pistols and clad in the field-gray of the Munich *Reichswehr* to which they were attached. Hitler's speeches soon found a loud echo in the ranks of the *Freikorps*, the hastily-formed units of demobilized right-wing troops who had banded together on an *ad hoc* basis to smash riots, keep order in the streets and prevent Germany from becoming a Bolshevik regime. Such armed supporters might well have been sympathetic, but they certainly had no undying loyalty to the new movement. So, towards the end of 1920, a permanent and regular Nazi formation called the *Saalschutz*, or Hall Guard, was set up to protect speakers at NSDAP meetings. In November 1921, the various Saalschutz groups throughout Bavaria were consolidated by the Freikorps leader Ernst Röhm and renamed *Sturmabteilungen*, or SA, after the élite German Army assault detachments of World War I. In return for securing the organizing abilities of Röhm and other military sponsors, Hitler had to let his 'party

PREVIOUS PAGES: Hitler consecrating new SS battalion flags at the Nürnberg Party Rally in 1933.

ABOVE: Ernst Röhm, Stabschef of the SA, whose organizational skill helped make possible Hitler's rise to power.

LEFT: Himmler, still wearing Obergruppenführer insignia, meeting army officers shortly before the Night of the Long Knives. He is accompanied by Karl Wolff, Reinhard Heydrich and Hans Prützmann.

ABOVE RIGHT: Freikorps troops manning an armored car in Berlin, spring 1919. The death's head, formerly used by imperial panzer units, was adopted by a number of Freikorps formations.

RIGHT: Freiherr von Manteuffel and men of his Baltic Freikorps in Riga, April 1919. Such troops would later provide eager volunteers for the SS.

ABOVE: Nazis on the march in 1922. Note the early flags with 'static' swastikas. Many SA men during this period simply retained the uniforms they had worn during the 1914-18 war, stripped of insignia and with the addition of swastika armbands.

LEFT: Hitler and Röhm inspecting massed ranks of Sturmabteilungen at Nürnberg, September 1933. The rowdy SA was by then 40 times the size of the German Army.

ABOVE RIGHT: Julius Schreck, Hitler's chauffeur, as an SS-Standartenführer in 1933. Schreck was co-founder of the Stosstrupp Adolf Hitler, and was never far from the Führer's side until his death from meningitis in 1936.

RIGHT: Himmler, Hess, Gregor Strasser and Franz von Salomon surround Hitler at the Reichs Party Day in Nürnberg, August 1927. The black képis set Himmler and Hess apart as members of the SS.

troops' slip under the aegis of the Freikorps and Reichswehr. By the time it paraded at the first national rally of the NSDAP in January 1923, the SA numbered 6000 men in four regiments. In an effort better to control the rapidly growing organization, Hitler appointed the former air ace, Hermann Göring, to lead it, but Göring was naturally lazy and self-indulgent and the driving force behind the SA remained Röhm. Frustrated by Röhm's ambition and independence, which were upheld by the military, Hitler was compelled to set up yet another body of men, from outside the SA, which would be entirely devoted to him. Thus the SS was born.

In March 1923 Hitler ordered the formation of a Munich-based bodyguard known as the *Stabswache*, whose members swore an oath of loyalty to him personally. Two months later, to avoid confusion with

other SA units of the same name, the Stabswache was integrated into a new, 30-man squad called the *Stosstrupp Adolf Hitler*, led by Julius Schreck and Josef Berchtold. The Stosstrupp participated in the ill-fated Munich *Putsch* on 9 November 1923, when Hitler's attempt to seize power in Bavaria by force ended in disaster. During the episode, Stosstrupp member Ulrich Graf saved Hitler's life and was severely wounded in the process. His bravery that day left a lasting impression on the Nazi Führer.

Following the *Putsch*, the NSDAP was banned and the SA dissolved. On his release from prison in December 1924, Hitler began to rebuild his shattered party. In February 1925 the NSDAP was reconstituted and the SA reactivated in an unarmed form. However, there was still no national SA, which remained at that stage little more than a social club for young roughnecks. In March, on the advice of Schreck, Hitler recommended to local party leaders the setting up of small guard details to be known as *Schutzstaffeln*, or protection squads, a new term subject to none of the governmental prohibitions and not identified with the old Freikorps traditions. The *Schutzstaffel der NSDAP*, soon abbreviated to SS, was to comprise 10-man squads selected from the most reliable party members. Their sole purpose would be to protect Hitler and other Nazi leaders during their political campaigning throughout Germany. On 9 November 1925 the existence of the SS was officially proclaimed in a ceremony at the Munich Feldherrnhalle.

During the spring of 1926, 75 Schutzstaffeln were formed right across the country. A new *SS-Oberleitung*

was created and headed by Berchtold, with the self-styled title of *Reichsführer der SS*. However, he rapidly lost interest and in March 1927 relinquished his office to his deputy, Erhard Heiden. Despite the extension of its numbers and theoretical prestige, the SS remained a limited organization subordinated to the SA. The latter kept a jealous eye on SS expansion and local SA commanders consistently used the SS under their control for the most demeaning tasks, such as distributing propaganda leaflets and recruiting subscribers to the party newspaper, the *Völkischer Beobachter*. By the end of 1928, morale in the SS was at an all-time low and membership plummeted. Photographs dating from that period rarely show as many as 10 SS men together.

The watershed in the development of the SS can be traced to a single day – 6 January 1929. On that fateful date, Heinrich Himmler took command of the organization at a time when the SA was becoming increasingly rebellious. In April, the new Reichsführer obtained approval for a recruiting plan designed to create a truly elite body out of the SS, and by 1930 it had grown to a force of 2000 men, with its own officer corps. When the SA in northern Germany rebelled against Gauleiter Josef Goebbels and his bourgeois NSDAP hierarchy in Berlin, only the local SS under Oberführer Kurt Daluege remained loyal to Hitler. The revolt collapsed and Himmler was rewarded with his appointment as security chief of the NSDAP headquarters in Munich. In effect, he was made head of the party police.

The SS grew steadily during 1931-32 within the matrix of a rapidly expanding SA and NSDAP membership. Himmler kept busy changing and rechanging his

LEFT: A salute to the banners of Nazism, c. 1932. Amid the vast numbers of SA present, three SS men are formed up at the head of the parade. The seeds of SS élitism had already been sown.

BELOW LEFT: SS men prepare to set fire to a collection of placards and flags seized from Berlin Communists, March 1933. The early black uniforms feature slight differences in the cut and position of buttons. Shoulder straps have not yet been introduced, and one SS man still wears a képi.

ABOVE RIGHT: A group of Reichskriegsflagge Freikorps members behind the Bavarian War Ministry on 9 November 1923. From left to right in the foreground are: Weickert, Kitzinger, Himmler (with imperial war flag), Seidel-Dittmarsch and Röhm.

RIGHT: During the parliamentary elections of the summer of 1932, the NSDAP emerged as one of the strongest parties. Hitler hosted a celebratory gathering for his newest Reichstag members in Berlin's Hotel Kaiserhof, and among those present were von Ulrich, Heines, Himmler, Ritter von Epp and Röhm.

unit designations to keep up with the elaborate tables of organization being constructed by Röhm and his staff. By the summer of 1932, the SS numbered 450 officers and 25,000 men, with administrative units known as *Oberführer-Abschnitte* interposed between about 40 regiments and the Reichsführer-SS. During that year, the political struggle in Germany rapidly took on the form of a civil war. The Communists and Socialists set up armed militias and the SA and SS responded. Ten SS men were killed and several hundred wounded during running street battles with the Red Front. The whole scenario was lapped up by the SS Old Guard, and their catch-phrase, 'Die Kampfzeit war die beste Zeit' ('The fighting days were the best') was frequently repeated as a form of boast to young SS men years later during the Third Reich.

As the crucial 1933 elections approached, it suited the Nazis to create the impression that Germany was on the verge of anarchy and that they had all the solutions. It was perhaps not surprising that they won a great electoral victory, and on 30 January the old Field Marshal Paul von Hindenburg, President of the Reich and a sort of 'Ersatz Kaiser' (substitute emperor), entrusted Hitler with the post of Chancellor and the responsibility of forming a government. Less than a month later, the Reichstag building was burned to the ground and the Communists were blamed. Hitler immediately gave police powers to 25,000 SA and 15,000 SS men, and left-wing opponents of the new regime began to be arrested in large numbers and herded into makeshift prisons and camps. While the SS was consolidating its situation and controlling its membership and recruitment by a constant purging process, the SA began to throw its weight about noisily. Denied a position in the Nazi state to which it felt entitled, the SA talked of a 'Second Revolution' which would sweep away both the bourgeois of the party and the reactionaries of the Reichswehr. On 30 June 1934, the 'Night of the Long Knives', Röhm and the SA leadership were eliminated in operations carried out by the SS and the army.

On 20 July 1934, Hitler declared the 200,000-strong SS an independent formation of the NSDAP and removed it completely from SA control. Its position of ascendancy was now assured and it entered a period of consolidation; a new command structure and organization was developed under Himmler, whose rank as Reichsführer-SS for the first time actually meant what it implied and made him directly subordinate to Hitler. Under the SS High Command, or *Reichsführung-SS*, the following eight main departments, or *Hauptämter*, ultimately evolved for the purpose of carrying out the day-to-day work of directing and administering the organization.

The Hauptamt Persönlicher Stab RfSS
(Pers. Stab RfSS)

Himmler's personal staff, comprising specialist officials, advisers, honorary officers and administrative personnel.

The SS Hauptamt (SS-HA)

The SS Central Office, responsible for recruitment and the maintenance of records on non-commissioned SS men.

The SS Führungshauptamt (SS-FHA)

SS Operational Headquarters, which co-ordinated training, the payment of wages, the supply of equipment, arms, ammunition and vehicles, and the maintenance and repair of stocks.

OPPOSITE PAGE, TOP LEFT: 1933, Himmler and the senior SS leadership, a few of whom still wore the brownshirt and képi.

OPPOSITE PAGE, BOTTOM LEFT: Reverses of a Blood Order, awarded to Munich Putsch veterans and featuring the Feldherrnhalle monument, and a 25mm lapel-buttonhole version of the Golden Party Badge.

OPPOSITE PAGE, RIGHT: Himmler and Röhm in August 1933.

RIGHT: Röhm and his staff in 1933. The one-eyed Viktor Lutze, on Röhm's left, presided over the much weaker SA from 1934 until 1943.

BELOW: The Blood Order, shown here with its case and lapel miniature, and the Golden Party Badge were symbols of the Nazi Old Guard.

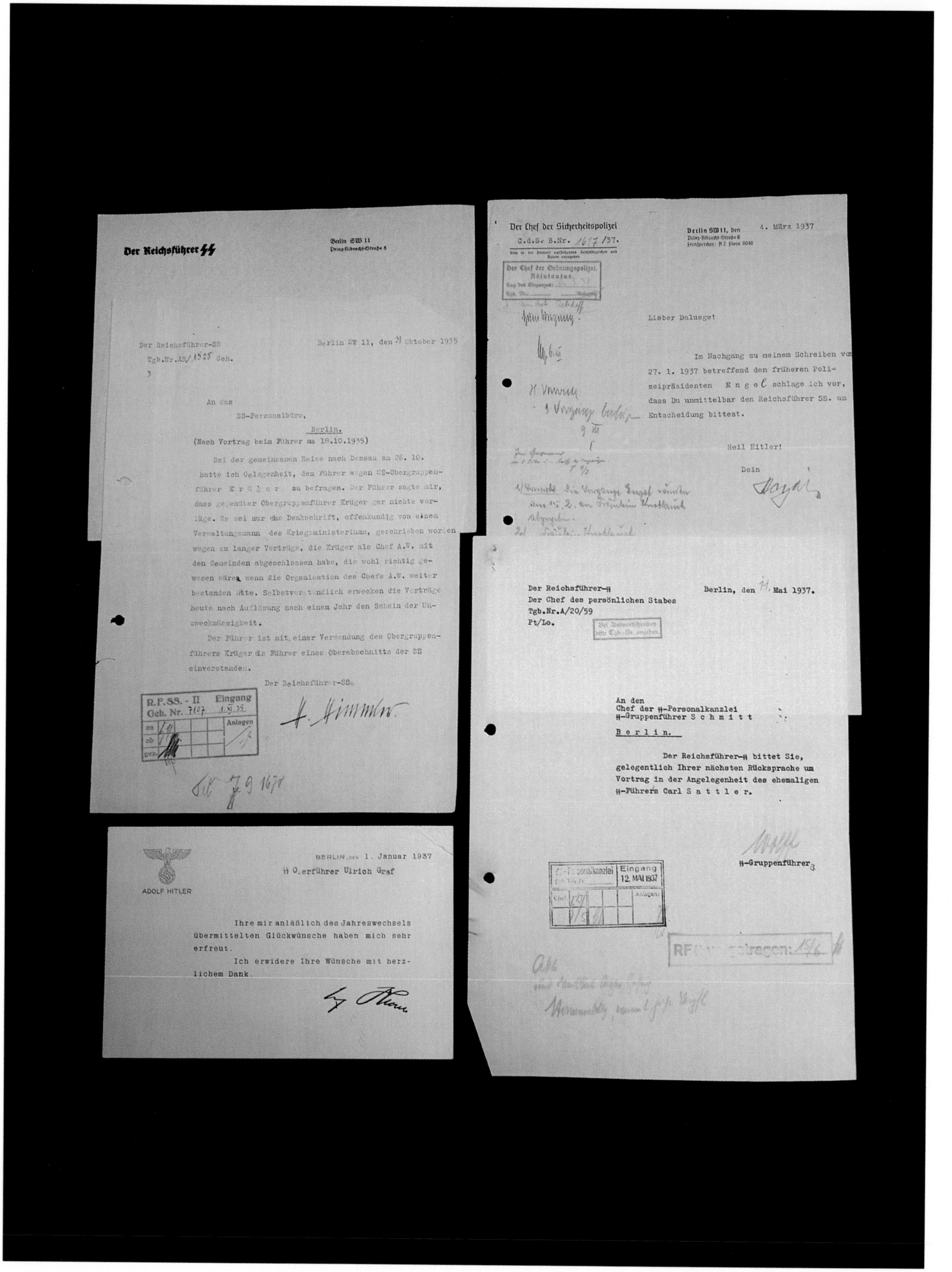

Der Reichsführer SS

Berlin SW 11
Prinz-Albrecht-Straße 8

Der Reichsführer-SS
Tgb.Nr.AR/1525 Geh.
3

Berlin SW 11, den 31 Oktober 1935

An das
SS-Personalbüro,
Berlin.

(Nach Vortrag beim Führer am 18.10.1935)

Bei der gemeinsamen Reise nach Dessau am 26. 10. hatte ich Gelegenheit, den Führer wegen SS-Obergruppenführer K r ü g e r zu befragen. Der Führer sagte mir, dass gegenüber Obergruppenführer Krüger gar nichts vorläge. Es sei nur die Denkschrift, offenkundig von einem Verwaltungsmann des Kriegsministeriums, geschrieben worden wegen zu langer Verträge, die Krüger als Chef A.W. mit den Gemeinden abgeschlossen habe, die wohl richtig gewesen wären, wenn die Organisation des Chefs A.W. weiter bestanden hätte. Selbstverständlich erwecken die Verträge heute nach Auflösung nach einem Jahr den Schein der Unzweckmässigkeit.

Der Führer ist mit einer Verwendung des Obergruppenführers Krüger als Führer eines Oberabschnitts der SS einverstanden.

Der Reichsführer-SS.
H. Himmler

R.F.SS. - II Eingang
Geh. Nr. 7107 1.XI.35

Der Chef der Sicherheitspolizei
C.d.S. B.Nr. 1617/37.

Der Chef der Ordnungspolizei.
Adjutantur.

Berlin SW 11, den 4. März 1937
Prinz-Albrecht-Straße 8
Fernsprecher: A 2 Flora 0040

Lieber Daluege!

Im Nachgang zu meinem Schreiben vom 27. 1. 1937 betreffend den früheren Polizeipräsidenten E n g e l schlage ich vor, dass Du unmittelbar den Reichsführer SS. um Entscheidung bittest.

Heil Hitler!

Dein
Heydrich

Der Reichsführer-SS
Der Chef des persönlichen Stabes
Tgb.Nr.A/20/59
Pt/Lo.

Berlin, den 11. Mai 1937.

Bei Antwortschreiben bitte Tgb.-Nr. angeben.

An den
Chef der SS-Personalkanzlei
SS-Gruppenführer S c h m i t t
B e r l i n.

Der Reichsführer-SS bittet Sie, gelegentlich Ihrer nächsten Rücksprache um Vortrag in der Angelegenheit des ehemaligen SS-Führers Carl S a t t l e r.

Wolff
SS-Gruppenführer

SS-Personalkanzlei Eingang 12. MAI 1937

RFSS eingetragen: 15/6

ADOLF HITLER

BERLIN, den 1. Januar 1937

SS Oberführer Ulrich Graf

Ihre mir anläßlich des Jahreswechsels übermittelten Glückwünsche haben mich sehr erfreut.

Ich erwidere Ihre Wünsche mit herzlichem Dank.

A. Hitler

LEFT: Documents signed by Himmler, his adjutant Wolff, and Heydrich are displayed beside a sheet of the Reichsführer's official headed notepaper and a New Year card from Adolf Hitler.

RIGHT: The SS newspaper *Das Schwarze Korps* alongside copies of *FM-Zeitschrift*, the magazine for SS patron members, and *Storm SS*, the periodical of the Germanic-SS in the Netherlands.

BELOW: An SS typewriter. Such machines, with runic SS keys, were introduced during the first half of 1936 for use in SS offices.

The Reichssicherheitshauptamt (RSHA)

The Reich's Central Security Office, controlling the security police of the Third Reich, including the Kripo, Gestapo and SD. It was also responsible for both foreign and domestic intelligence operations, espionage and counter-espionage, and combating political and common-law crime.

The SS Wirtschafts- und Verwaltungshauptamt (SS-WVHA)

The SS Economic and Administrative Department, which oversaw a large number of SS industrial and agricultural undertakings, administered the finances of the SS and ran the concentration camps.

The Rasse- und Siedlungshauptamt (RuSHA)

The Race and Settlement Department looked after the racial purity of all SS members and was responsible for executing the policy of settling SS men in the eastern territories.

The Hauptamt SS-Gericht (HA SS-Gericht)

The SS Legal Department administered the disciplinary side of the special code of laws to which members of the SS were subject.

The SS Personalhauptamt (Pers. HA)

The SS Personnel Department dealt with personnel matters and kept records on all SS officers.

Immediately below the Hauptämter were the SS *Oberabschnitte* (Regions) and *Abschnitte* (Districts), the bases of the SS territorial organization.

From 1933-34, the SS split into two distinct groups: the traditional *Allgemeine-SS*, which was basically part-time and fulfilled a police function; and the full-time military *Bewaffnete-SS*, or armed SS. Each had its own distinctive series of uniforms and regalia. Both branches shared, however, total loyalty and commitment to Hitler, relishing the obedience required of them as the Führer's bodyguard.

LEFT: SS patron members, the Fördernde Mitglieder, or FM, were ordinary citizens who bound themselves to pay a monthly contribution to SS funds in return for Himmler's protection. In effect, the FM organization became a sort of 'Nazi Freemasonry', through which members could secure employment, business deals and promotion. When enrolled, each patron was presented with a membership book and lapel badge, and took out a subscription to the *FM-Zeitschrift*. This particular issue of the magazine features a cover photograph of the equestrian SS-Obersturmführer Gunther Temme and his horse 'Nordland', recent stars of the Berlin Olympics.

RIGHT: The SD attracted many intellectuals into its ranks. These identity documents relate to Dr Max Werner, who served with the Security Police in Wiesbaden. The Gestapo warrant disk below gave the bearer unlimited powers of access and arrest.

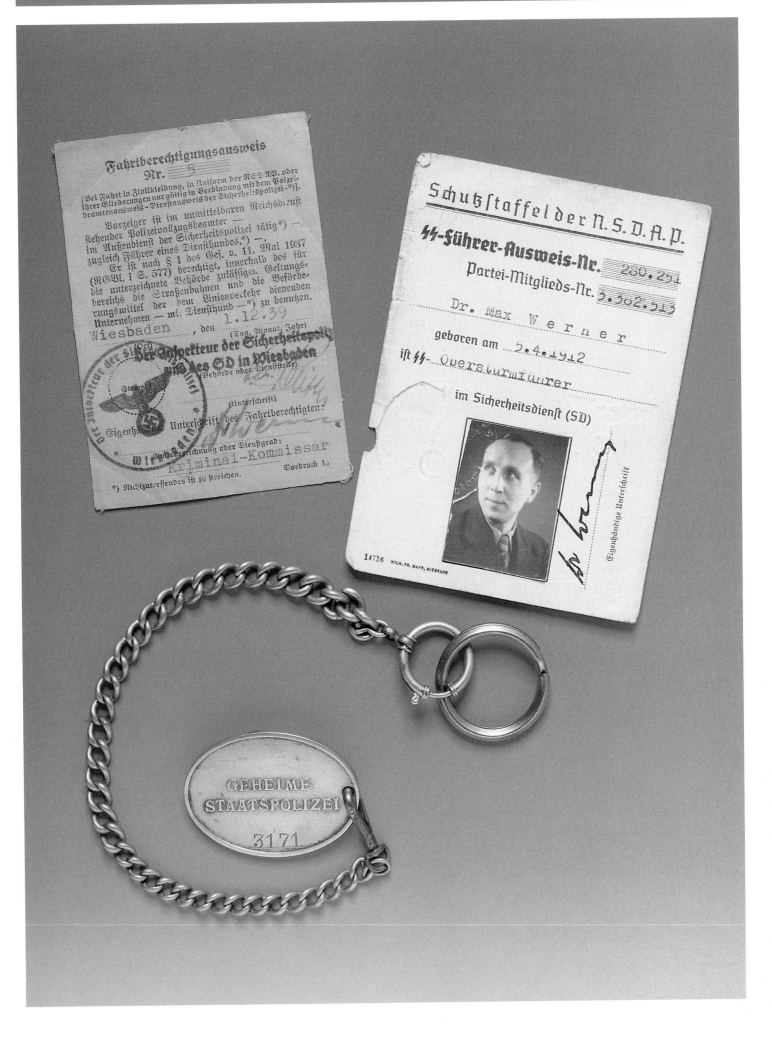

THE ALLGEMEINE-SS

The first and foremost duty of the entire SS organization was always the protection of Adolf Hitler. After the advent of the Leibstandarte, however, whose members worked full-time to a rota system and accompanied Hitler on his journeys throughout the Reich, the part-time SS men who had originally been recruited on a local basis to protect the Führer during his trips around Germany found that aspect of their work effectively taken from them. Consequently, it was decided that as of 1934 the main day-to-day function of these highly disciplined Allgemeine-SS volunteers would be to support the police in maintaining public order. The Nazi position in 1934-35 was far from secure, and the Allgemeine-SS rapidly expanded with the formation of many new units trained and equipped to combat any counter-revolution. The typical SS infantry regiment, or *Fuss-Standarte*, comprised 2000 men organized into active and reserve battalions (*Sturmbanne*), companies (*Stürme*), platoons (*Truppen*), sections (*Scharen*) and files (*Rotten*). These were supported by a vast array of specialists, including cavalry regiments (*Reiterstandarten*), signals battalions (*Nachrichtensturmbanne*), engineer battalions (*Pioniersturmbanne*), medical companies (*Sanitätsstürme*), a flying company (*Fliegersturm*) and a supplementary reserve (*Stammabteilung*). It was planned that, in the event of any internal uprising, the Allgemeine-SS would take over the operation of the post office, national radio network, public utilities and public transport, as well as acting as police reinforcements. However, the anticipated civil unrest never came about, and so the duties of the Allgemeine-SS before the outbreak of war in 1939 were

PREVIOUS PAGES: Hitler returns from Italy, 10 May 1938. The photograph was taken at Munich station.

ABOVE: Hitler arriving at Tempelhof arena in Berlin on Labor Day, 1 May 1934. Note the differences in cut of the SS service tunics, which had still not been fully standardized almost two years after their introduction.

LEFT: Hitler supports NSDAP-member General Karl Litzmann on the latter's 85th birthday in 1934, while inspecting a Leibstandarte guard of honor.

RIGHT: Hitler addressed a crowd of over one million at the Tempelhof arena, 1934. His Leibstandarte bodyguard detachment was commanded by SS-Hauptsturmführer Wilhelm Mohnke, (center) who was to achieve notoriety when he ordered the massacre of 50 British prisoners-of-war in 1940.

LEFT: Hitler greets 'der Treue Heinrich' at Führer Headquarters, Rastenburg, on 7 October 1943, while Martin Bormann lurks in the background. Himmler sports the Pilot-Observer Badge in Gold with Diamonds, which was a personal gift from Göring.

BELOW: Disabled servicemen competing on the games field during their convalescence, 28 March 1942. The man on the right wears SS sports kit, with Sig-Runen on the vest.

RIGHT: A selection of documents including Allgemeine-SS identity cards, a Waffen-SS Soldbuch and an FM membership book. The two 'death cards' at lower right commemorate SS men killed in battle, and were distributed by their families to friends.

generally restricted to overseeing crowd control at party rallies and other celebrations, including national holidays and state visits of foreign dignitaries.

The close relationship between the SS and police grew apace after Himmler was appointed Chef der Deutschen Polizei in June 1936. The Reichsführer planned to merge the two bodies into a single State Protection Corps or *Staatsschutzkorps*, which was to be achieved first by reorganization and then by the absorption of police personnel into the Allgemeine-SS. Throughout the remainder of the Third Reich, a large number of politically reliable and racially suitable policemen were granted SS membership, being taken into the Stammabteilung with SS ranks equivalent to their police status. Himmler ultimately succeeded in achieving control of all conventional German police forces, the fire brigade, railway and post office guards, rescue and emergency services, intelligence agencies and even night watchmen. Moreover, all the corresponding domestic police forces in the conquered countries, including the British Constabulary serving on the Channel Islands, came under his authority. Through their direction of these agencies, with their vast resources and intimate local knowledge, the Allge-meine-SS hierarchy exercized a power and influence more widespread and effective than anything contemplated by their fighting comrades in the Waffen-SS during World War II.

Allgemeine-SS members who were engaged in reserved occupations which prevented their call-up in 1939 took an active role in the war effort at home. In many cities, special SS *Wachkompanie* and *Alarmstürme* were detailed to protect factories, bridges, roads and other strategic points and assist the *Luftschutz* or Civil Defense during air raids. Some SS men worked as auxiliaries with the Customs Service while others helped with the harvest, supervized foreign laborers and engaged in welfare work. During 1944-45, the cadres of the Allgemeine-SS, spread throughout Germany, co-ordinated the organization of the *Volkssturm*, or Home Guard, which came under Himmler's control.

Conditions of service in the Allgemeine-SS high-lighted the élite nature of the organization. Recruiting was always strictly controlled, even during the war, with most young SS men coming directly from the ranks of the Hitler Youth. The latter worked hand-in-glove with the SS, and adopted many of its uniform accouterments and rituals. Selection was based on

LEFT: In 1933 50 Nazi couples were married in a mass service which took place in the Church of Lazarus in Berlin.

BELOW LEFT: An SS marriage permit and three SS bookplates. The SS Engagement and Marriage Order, dating from 1931, dictated that all members of the SS had to obtain Himmler's written permission to marry, which could be refused on racial or physical grounds.

RIGHT: An oak casket carved with Sig-Runes, a swastika, a Hagall-Rune, oakleaves and acorns. It was used as a container for the presentation copies of *Mein Kampf* which every newly-married couple received.

BELOW: An SS 'Christening' ceremony being conducted by an offical of the Rasse- und Siedlungshauptamt in 1936. The child is wrapped in a shawl of undyed wool embroidered with oakleaves, runes and swastikas.

racial purity, good health and a disciplined character, and training was carried out over a three-year period, with statutory breaks for obligatory service in the armed forces or *Reichsarbeitsdienst*. The confirmed SS man remained in the active Allgemeine-SS until he was 35 years old, after which he could transfer to one of the SS reserve units. Promotion was awarded on merit, and a strict SS legal and disciplinary code governed the behavior of every SS member. Ultimately, SS men were answerable only to special SS and police courts for any crimes and offenses they committed, and were in effect put above the normal jurisdiction of the civil courts. The same racial qualities looked for in the SS man were also required of his wife, and Christian weddings were replaced by neo-pagan ceremonies for the Allgemeine-SS, with couples expected to raise at least four children.

The Allgemeine-SS eventually outgrew its police function and came to have a wide-ranging effect on all aspects of life throughout Nazi Germany. The racial policies of the Third Reich were put into operation through SS agencies, primarily the *Reichskommissariat für die Festigung des deutschen Volkstums*, or RKFDV, the Reich Commission for the Consolidation of Germanism, which organized the resettlement of racial

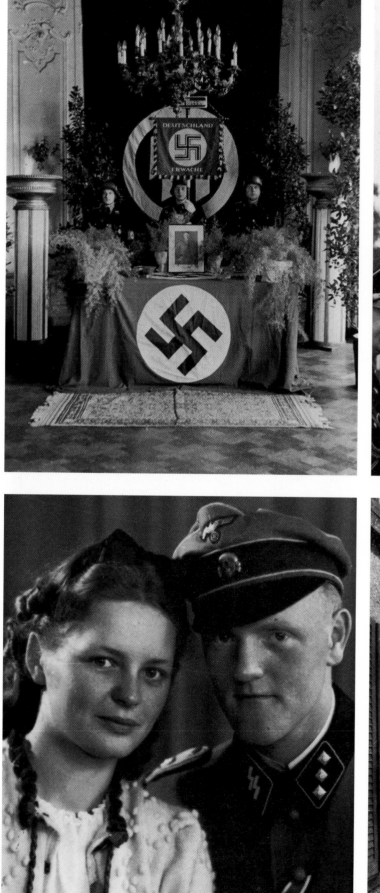

OPPOSITE PAGE, LEFT: An SS altar, prepared for a wedding or child-naming ceremony in 1936. The pseudo-pagan rites of the Allgemeine-SS became ever more complex as the Third Reich progressed, and were designed to enhance the mystique of Himmler's Black Order.

OPPOSITE PAGE, RIGHT: Wolff, Himmler and Hess enjoying a joke at the entrance to Dachau concentration camp in 1935.

OPPOSITE PAGE, BELOW LEFT: Wartime newly-weds.

OPPOSITE PAGE, BELOW RIGHT: Lebensborn homes were financed by contributions from SS officers and the FM organization.

RIGHT: The SS and the German police were intended to be merged at the earliest feasible opportunity, and the ubiquitous Sig-Runes featured on the bulletins and newspapers of both organizations.

German repatriates in the occupied eastern territories. Another SS group, the *Volksdeutsche Mittelstelle* or VOMI, played a significant part in paving the way for the Nazi occupation of Austria and Czechoslovakia. In an effort to prove the racial hypotheses of National Socialism by scientific means, Himmler set up Ahnenerbe, a body for the research of ancestral heritage. The SS duly carried out archaeological excavations throughout Europe in the search for the origins of the Nordic race, a study which ultimately resulted in human experimentation using concentration camp inmates.

The concentration camp system also gave the SS access to an unlimited supply of cheap expendable labor, which led to a thriving SS economy. Various manufacturing enterprises were set up in the camps, and workers leased out to private firms on sub-contract. The acquisition of large fertile territories during the war greatly enlarged the scope of these activities. Farming and stockbreeding in Poland, and lumbering, mining and fishing in Russia all entered the field of SS economics, and between 1941 and 1944 the SS exploited the wealth, resources and population of the conquered East on a massive scale. Himmler eventually controlled over 500 factories, producing 75 per cent of Germany's soft drinks and 95 per cent of the country's furniture. Most of the uniforms and equipment used by the SS and police were manufactured in the camps, whose inmates also baked bread, processed meat, made munitions and repaired leather goods. The SS ran quarries, brickworks, cement factories, food research laboratories, a publishing house, a sword smithy and even a porcelain works. The money which flowed into SS coffers as a result was vast, and helped to strengthen Himmler's position and maintain the financial autonomy of his organization.

Through its industrial connections, the Allgemeine-SS cultivated and recruited hundreds of company directors, businessmen and landowners. Others became SS patron members, making regular donations to SS funds in return for Himmler's favor and protection. By means of a thorough policy of infiltration, the SS duly permeated right through every branch of official and semi-official German life. By May 1944, no less than 25 per cent of the leading personalities in Germany were members of the Allgemeine-SS, some being regulars and others so-called *'Ehrenführer'* or honorary officers. They included almost all of Hitler's immediate entourage, men in key party and government posts, top civil servants, members of the military aristocracy, doctors, scientists, university professors and those prominent in the fields of culture and charitable works. After the failed plot to assassinate Hitler in July 1944, the SS finally overcame that last bastion of the old traditional Germany, the army, with SS generals taking over the military administration and secret weapons program. By the end of 1944, the Allgemeine-SS had seized almost total political, military and economic power in Germany.

The uniforms and regalia of the Allgemeine-SS developed as the organization expanded, and will now be covered in some detail.

MEINE HERZLICHSTEN
GLÜCKWÜNSCHE ZUM WEIHNACHTSFEST
UND
FÜR DAS KRIEGSJAHR 1945

HEIL HITLER!

H. Himmler.

REICHSFÜHRER-SS

ABOVE LEFT: A Christmas greetings card sent by Himmler at the end of 1944.

ABOVE: One of the earthenware Julleuchter candleholders which were distributed annually to selected SS men on the occasion of the winter solstice.

LEFT: The SS porcelain and ceramics factory at Allach, near Munich, was part of the Dachau concentration-camp complex and produced fine quality pieces. Its trademark was two interlocked Sig-Runes. This figure of Athena commemorated the Day of German Art in 1938.

RIGHT: This exquisitely formed porcelain basset-hound puppy was a popular Allach product, and is shown overlooking a model SS man in traditional uniform. A range of toy soldiers of this type were manufactured by the firms of Elastolin and Lineol for the mass market during the 1930s.

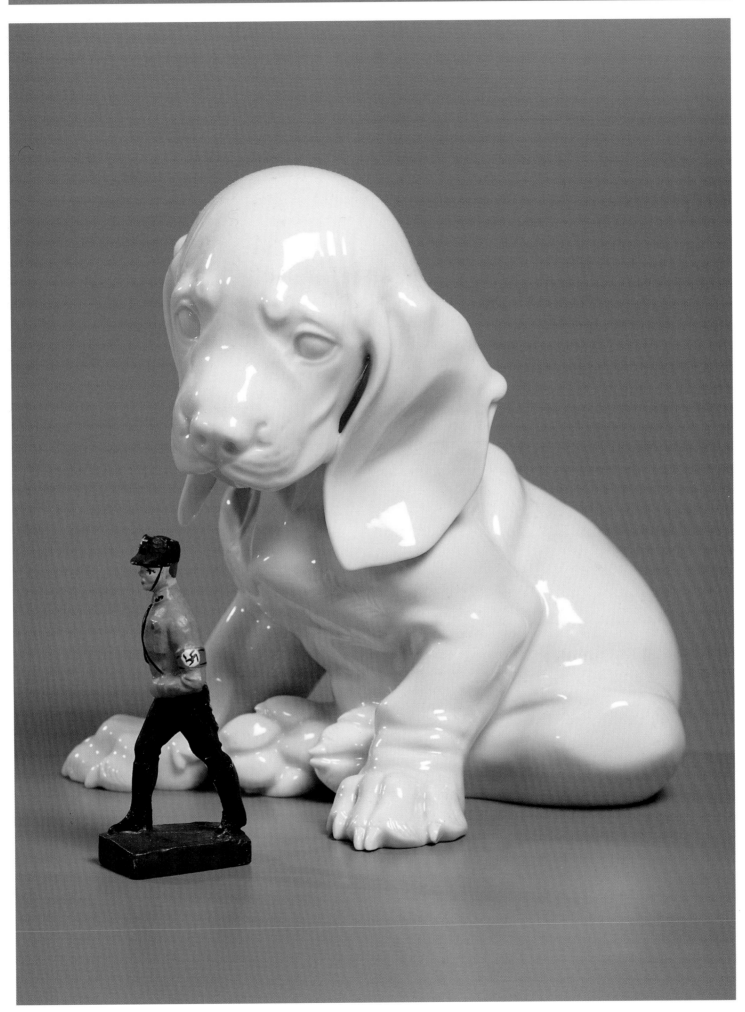

The Death's Head

Of all SS uniform trappings and accouterments, the one emblem which endured throughout the history of the organization and became firmly associated with it was the death's head, or *Totenkopf*, an eerie motif comprising a skull and crossed bones. It has often been assumed that the death's head was adopted simply to strike terror into the hearts of those who saw it. However, that was not so. It was chosen as a direct and emotional link with the past, and in particular with the élite military units of the Imperial Reich.

Medieval German literature and romantic poems were filled with references to dark forces and the symbols of death and destruction. In 1740, a large right-facing jawless death's head with the bones lying behind the skull, embroidered in silver bullion, adorned the black funeral trappings of the Prussian King, Frederick William I. In his memory, the Leib-Husaren Regiments Nos. 1 and 2, élite Prussian royal bodyguard units which were formed the following year, took black as the color of their uniforms and wore a massive Totenkopf of similar design on their Pelzmützen or busbies. The State of Brunswick followed suit in 1809 when the death's head was adopted by its Hussar Regiment No. 17 and the third battalion of Infantry Regiment No. 92. The Brunswick Totenkopf differed slightly in design from the Prussian one, with the skull facing forward and situated directly above the crossed bones. During World War I the death's head was chosen as a formation sign by a number of crack German army units, particu-larly the storm troops, flamethrower detachments and tank battalions. After 1918 the death's head surfaced again on the streets of Germany, this time painted on the helmets and vehicles of certain Freikorps. Because of its association with these formations, the Totenkopf became symbolic not only of wartime daring and self-sacrifice but also of postwar traditionalism, anti-Liberalism and anti-Bolshevism.

It is not surprising, therefore, that members of the Stosstrupp Adolf Hitler eagerly took the Totenkopf as their distinctive emblem in 1923, initially acquiring a small stock of appropriate army surplus cap badges. Their successors in the SS thereafter contracted the firm of Deschler in Munich to restrike large quantities of the Prussian-style jawless death's head which they used on their headgear for the next 11 years. In 1934, when the Prussian Totenkopf began to be worn as an élite badge by the new army panzer units, the SS devised its own unique pattern of grinning death's head, with lower jaw, which it used thereafter until the SS's demise in 1945.

The 1934-pattern SS Totenkopf ultimately took various forms, right-facing, left-facing and front-facing, and appeared on the cloth headgear of all SS members. It was the centerpiece of the SS Death's Head Ring and could be seen on dagger and gorget suspension chains, mess jackets, flags, standards, drum covers and trumpet banners. Himmler wanted his men to be proud of their heritage and there is no doubt that the historical associations of the death's head were well used to that end.

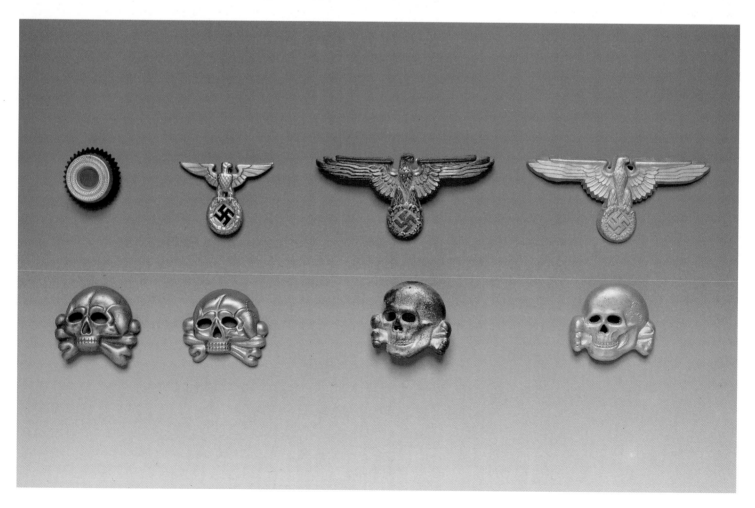

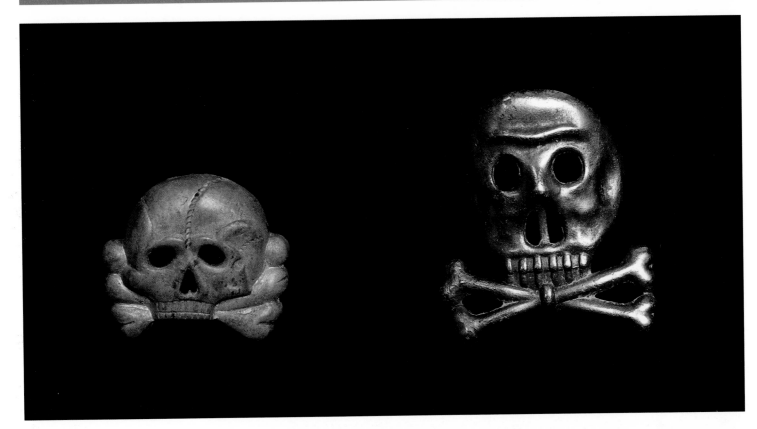

LEFT: SS cap insignia evolved steadily between 1923 and 1945. The Reich cockade gave way to the small NSDAP eagle during the fall of 1929, and in 1934 the Prussian Totenkopf was replaced by the distinctive SS pattern with lower jaw. The definitive SS eagle first appeared in 1936, and like the grinning death's head, was initially manufactured in silver-plated Tombakbronze, then aluminum and finally zinc-based alloys.

ABOVE: Death's heads were not worn solely by the SS during the Third Reich. The Prussian style on the left was used by the army's 5th cavalry regiment, while the (Braunschweig) Brunswick pattern, right, was sported by members of the 17th infantry regiment. Panzer units, the naval Kustenschütz Danzig and the Luftwaffe's Schleppgruppe 4 and Kampfgruppe 54 all chose the Totenkopf as their distinctive emblem.

RIGHT: An Austrian 1916-pattern steel helmet with hand-painted death's head, as worn by various Freikorps formations c. 1919-20.

The Runes

Alongside the Totenkopf, the SS runes represented the élitism and brotherly comradeship of the organization, and were consciously elevated to an almost holy status. They derived from the characters which formed the alphabets used by the Germanic tribes of pre-Christian Europe, and particularly appealed to Himmler's vision of the SS as a chivalric order, and to his fascination for cryptic codes and hidden messages.

All pre-1939 Allgemeine-SS men were instructed in runic symbolism as part of their probationary training. By 1945, 14 main varieties of rune were in use by the SS, and these are described from A to N below and shown in the accompanying illustrations. The finer points of these runes were never generally appreciated by the majority of men who wore them, and instruction in their meanings ceased around 1940.

LEFT: A selection of SS collar patches. These are, from left to right, top to bottom:
(i) Runic patch worn initially only by the Leibstandarte and then, from 1940, by all German and Germanic units of the Waffen-SS not allocated other patches. This example is hand-embroidered in silver bullion for officers, with the piping removed for field use.
(ii) As above, but machine-woven in silver thread for officers.
(iii) As above, but machine-embroidered for other ranks.
(iv) As above, but machine-woven for other ranks.
(v) Hand-embroidered patch worn by a member of the 63rd Fuss-Standarte (Tübingen) of the Allgemeine-SS. Early examples were often made without piping of any sort.
(vi) As above, but for the 1st Fuss-Standarte 'Julius Schreck' (Munich), and with other ranks' piping.
(vii) Patch worn by an officer of the 113th Fuss-Standarte (Kalisch), based in occupied Poland.
(viii) Patch for an officer on the staff of SS Oberabschnitt Ost.

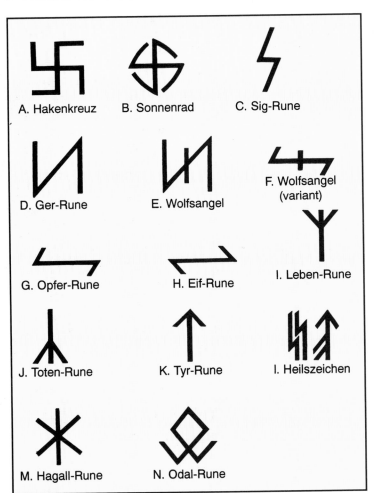

A. Hakenkreuz B. Sonnenrad C. Sig-Rune

D. Ger-Rune E. Wolfsangel F. Wolfsangel (variant)

G. Opfer-Rune H. Eif-Rune I. Leben-Rune

J. Toten-Rune K. Tyr-Rune I. Heilszeichen

M. Hagall-Rune N. Odal-Rune

A The Hakenkreuz

The Hakenkreuz or swastika was the pagan Germanic sign of Donner (or Thor), the Thunder God. A very similar symbol was common in Hindu culture, although the hooks faced to the left. Hindu legend stated that reversing the swastika would bring bad luck to the instigator. During the nineteenth century it came to be regarded as symbolic of nationalism, and in the post-1918 period was adopted by the Ehrhardt Brigade and other Freikorps units. As the senior badge of the Nazi party and state, it inevitably featured on many SS accouterments, either static (i.e. standing flat) or mobile (i.e. standing on one point to give the appearance of an advancing movement).

B The Sonnenrad

The Sonnenrad or sunwheel swastika was the old Norse representation of the sun.

C The Sig-Rune

The Sig-Rune (also known as the Siegrune) was symbolic of victory. Around 1932 SS man Walter Heck, a graphic designer employed by the badge manufacturing firm of Ferdinand Hoffstätter in Bonn, drew two Sig-Runes side by side and thus created the ubiquitous 'SS-Runen' used thereafter by all branches of the organization. The SS paid him 2.50 Reichsmarks for the rights to his design!

D The Ger-Rune

The Ger-Rune was symbolic of communal spirit.

E The Wolfsangel

The Wolfsangel, or Wolf Hook, was originally a pagan device which supposedly possessed the magical power to ward off wolves. It was adopted as an emblem by less superstitious fifteenth-century peasants in their revolt against the mercenaries of the German princes, and was thereafter regarded as representing liberty and independence.

F The Wolfsangel (variant)

A squat version of the Wolfsangel with hooked arms was worn as an early badge of the NSDAP, and was later adopted by the Dutch SS.

G The Opfer-Rune

The Opfer-Rune symbolized self-sacrifice, and commemorated the Nazi martyrs of the 1923 Munich Putsch.

H The Eif-Rune

The Eif-Rune represented zeal and enthusiasm. It was the early insignia of specially-selected SS adjutants assigned personally to Hitler and, as such, was worn by Rudolf Hess in 1929.

I The Leben-Rune

The Leben-Rune or Life Rune symbolized life and was adopted by the SS Lebensborn Society, which ran maternity homes. It likewise featured on SS documents and graves to show date of birth.

J The Toten-Rune

The Toten-Rune or Death Rune represented death, and was used on documents and graves to show date of death.

K The Tyr-Rune

The Tyr-Rune, also known as the Kampf-Rune or Battle Rune, was the pagan Germanic sign of Tyr, the God of War, and was symbolic of leadership in battle. It was commonly used by the SS as a grave marker, replacing the Christian cross, and a Tyr-Rune worn on the upper left arm indicated graduation from the SA Reichsführerschule, which trained SS officers until 1934. It was later the specialist badge of the SS recruiting and training department.

L The Heilszeichen

The Heilszeichen or Prosperity Symbols represented success and good fortune, and appeared on the SS Death's Head Ring.

M The Hagall-Rune

The Hagall-Rune stood for the unshakable faith (in Nazi philosophy) which was expected of all SS members. It featured on numerous ceremonial accouterments, particularly those used at weddings.

N The Odal-Rune

The Odal-Rune symbolized kinship and family and the bringing together of people of similar blood. It was the badge of the SS Race and Settlement Department.

The Traditional Uniform

The earliest Nazis wore normal civilian clothing and were distinguished only by their crudely hand-made *Kampfbinde*, or swastika armbands, worn on the left upper arm. With the advent of the paramilitary SA in 1921, however, it became necessary to evolve a uniform specifically for its members. At first, their dress lacked any consistency and was characteristically Freikorps in style, generally taking the form of field-gray army surplus double-breasted windcheater jackets, waist belts with cross-straps, gray trousers, trench boots, mountain caps and steel helmets. Many SA men simply retained the uniforms they had worn during World War I, stripped of badges. The swastika armband was the only constant feature, sometimes bearing a metal numeral or emblem to indicate unit identity, and a metal 'pip' or cloth stripes to denote rank. In 1923, members of the Stabswache and Stosstrupp Adolf Hitler wore similar garb with the addition of a Prussian-pattern death's head on the cap, usually surmounted by the *Reichskokarde*, a circular metal cockade in the Imperial colors of black, white and red. After the failure of the Munich Putsch and the banning of the SA and Stosstrupp, the men continued to wear their old uniforms of the clandestine 'Frontbanne', adding a steel helmet badge to the center of the swastika armband.

At the end of 1924, Gerhard Rossbach, a former SA officer, acquired a bargain lot of surplus German Army tropical brown shirts in Austria. These items were, in reality, not shirts at all but blouses with collars and

LEFT: Uniform of the Stosstrupp Adolf Hitler, 1923. It is basically Reichsheer in character, with a swastika armband and Austrian-Army-pattern cap. Although the Stosstrupp had no formalized rank structure, a white horizontal stripe through the center of the armband denoted the wearer's general position as squad leader.

BELOW LEFT: The regulation SS swastika armband with black borders dated from 1925, and was ultimately produced in a variety of sizes and qualities for wear on the shirt, tunic and greatcoat by officers and other ranks. During the spring of 1933 it was used in conjunction with a selection of 'Hilfspolizei' brassards by the 15,000 SS men sworn in as auxiliary policemen following the burning of the Reichstag.

RIGHT: A variety of civilian and quasi-military windcheater jackets were worn by the SS in inclement weather during 1925-26. By this time, the black SS képi had made its appearance, and a range of NSDAP and SA belt buckles was also being produced.

pockets which were worn over an ordinary collarless shirt. When the NSDAP and SA were reconstituted during the spring of 1925, Hitler kitted his men out with these readily available shirts and had ties, breeches and képis made to match. So by chance circumstances rather than design, brown became the adopted color of the SA and the Nazi party in general.

When the SS was formed in April of the same year, its members too were issued with brown shirts. To distinguish them from the SA, however, they retained their death's heads and wore black képis, black ties, black breeches and black borders to the swastika armband. By the end of 1925 the brown shirt with black accouterments was firmly established as the so-called 'traditional uniform' of the SS. The vast majority of SS men who were also members of the NSDAP wore the Nazi party badge on their ties.

On 9 November 1926, the rapidly expanding SA introduced collar patches or *Kragenspiegel* to indicate unit and rank, replacing the badges and stripes formerly worn on the armband. The right patch bore unit numerals and the left patch a system of rank pips, bars and oakleaves. In August 1929, the SS followed suit with a simplified series of black and silver patches. Unlike their complex and multi-colored SA counterparts, SS unit patches did not indicate Sturmbann or Sturm identity, which was instead shown on narrow black bands known as cuff titles worn on the lower left sleeve.

LEFT: A 1933 Standartenführer's uniform. Note the senior officer's képi with piping, the newly-introduced shoulder strap, and the Tyr-Rune on the upper left sleeve, denoting graduation from the SA-Reichsführerschule.

BELOW LEFT: A Leibstandarte battalion parades past Hitler on his 49th birthday, 20 April 1938.

ABOVE: This unique tunic is purported to have been worn in 1928 by Franz Xaver Schwarz, Treasurer of the NSDAP, four years before the introduction of the black SS service uniform. A veteran of the Munich Putsch, Schwarz was very close to Himmler who made him the highest ranking General in the entire SS, second only to the Reichsführer. In return, Schwarz ensured that the Allgemeine-SS received all the financial backing it required, often at the expense of other Party branches like the SA and NSFK.

RIGHT: Black service uniform as worn by an SS-Oberscharführer in the 12th Sturm, 3rd Sturmbann, 88th SS Fuss-Standarte (Bremen), c.1935. The 'swallow's nests' at the shoulders denote his position as a member of the unit's drum corps, and his decorations, including the Turkish War Star, indicate extensive World War I service.

Within every Fuss-Standarte, each Sturmbann was assigned a color which bordered the upper and lower edges of the cuff title. The prescribed Sturmbann colors were:

Sturmbann I – Green
Sturmbann II – Dark Blue
Sturmbann III – Red
Sturmbann IV (Reserve) – Light Blue

The number and, if appropriate, honor name of the wearer's Sturm appeared embroidered in gray or silver thread on the title. Thus a member of the 2nd Sturm, 1st Sturmbann, 41st SS Fuss-Standarte would wear a green-bordered cuff title bearing the numeral '2' in conjunction with the number '41' on his right collar patch. A man in the 11th Sturm 'Adolf Höh', 3rd Sturmbann, 30th SS Fuss-Standarte would sport a red-edged cuff title with the legend '11 Adolf Höh', and regimental numeral '30' on the right collar patch. All members of Allgemeine-SS cavalry units had yellow-edged cuff titles while those of signals and pioneer formations had their titles bordered in brown and black, respectively. A relatively small number of cuff titles bore Roman numerals or designations relating to staff or specialist appointments.

During the autumn of 1929, a small sharp-winged eagle and swastika badge, or *Hoheitsabzeichen*, was introduced for wear on the SA and SS képi in place of the Reichskokarde. SS bandsmen's uniforms were further modified by the addition of black-and-white military-style 'swallow's nests' worn at the shoulder.

At the end of 1931, the SS adopted the motto, 'Meine Ehre heisst Treue' ('My Honor is Loyalty') following a well-publicized open letter from Hitler to Kurt Daluege after the collapse of the northern SA revolt, declaring in his praise: 'SS Mann, deine Ehre heisst Treue'. Almost immediately, a belt buckle incorporating the motto into its design was commissioned and produced by the Overhoff firm of Lüdenscheid to replace the SA buckle hitherto worn by all members of the SS. The new belt buckle was circular for officers and rectangular for other ranks, and continued in wear unchanged until 1945.

In May 1933, shoulder straps or *Achselstücke* were devised for wear on the right shoulder only. These straps were adornments to be used in conjunction with the collar insignia already in existence and indicated rank level (i.e. enlisted man or NCO, junior officer or intermediate officer etc.) rather than actual rank.

In February 1934, a silver Honor Chevron for the Old Guard (*Ehrenwinkel für Alte Kämpfer*) was authorized for wear on the upper right arm by all members of the SS who had joined the SS, NSDAP or any of the other party-affiliated organizations prior to 30 January 1933. The Honor Chevron came to be regarded as the badge of the 'die-hard' Nazi, even although an 18-year-old SS recruit in 1939 would have been entitled to wear it had he been a 10-year-old Hitler Youth in 1931. Qualification was later extended even further to include former members of the police or armed forces who fulfilled certain conditions and transferred into the SS.

The traditional brown shirt uniform of the SS therefore developed almost continually over 11 years and incorporated many additions or alterations at specific times. These can be of great assistance in dating period photographs. With the advent of the black uniform, the traditional uniform was gradually phased out and it was not generally worn after 1934, except on special ceremonial occasions by members of the SS Old Guard.

LEFT: Service tunic of a Sturmbannführer on the staff of the Pomeranian SA. The cuff title on the right sleeve, above the SA service stripes, was introduced on 25 May 1936 as a commemorative award for the 30 or so veterans of the Stosstrupp Adolf Hitler. 'Old Guard' status is reinforced by the Blood Order ribbon and Golden Party Badge.

RIGHT: The Honor Chevron of the Old Guard was produced with black, gray-green and white borders for wear on SS, police and summer uniforms. It was proudly borne on every possible occasion by those entitled to use it, and was presented together with a certificate.

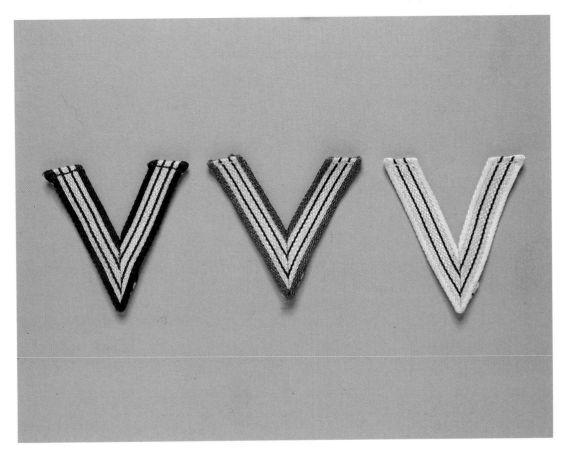

LEFT: Allgemeine-SS man's Schirmmütze, *c.* 1935.

BELOW: A selection of caps showing the development of SS headgear. From left to right: Austrian-Army-pattern képi dating from 1923; black SS képi introduced in 1925; formalized képi used from 1929; peaked cap *c.* 1936.

RIGHT: Arm diamonds worn to acknowledge specialist skills or to signify membership of selected SS departments. From left to right, top to bottom: transport NCO, medical orderly, farrier, buildings administrator, administrative officer, cavalryman, Race and Settlement official, Recruiting and Training official, armorer NCO, signaler.

The Black Uniform

A major change to SS uniform was made in 1932, in response to a government demand that the SA and SS should adopt a more 'respectable' outfit as a condition of the lifting of a ban on political uniforms. On 7 July a black tunic and peaked cap, harking back to the garb of the Imperial Leib-Husaren, were introduced for the SS, replacing the brown shirt and képi. These items were made available first to officers, then lower ranks, and were worn side-by-side with the traditional uniform during 1933 while all members were being kitted out.

The new SS uniform was designed by SS-Oberführer Prof. Dr. Karl Diebitsch. The tunic comprised a standard four-pocket military-style jacket, the lower two pockets being of the slanted 'slash' type, with a four-button front. There were two belt hooks at the sides and two false buttons at the rear to support the leather waist belt. Insignia was the same as that devised for the traditional uniform, and the tunic was worn over a plain brown shirt. The new SS peaked caps were again military in appearance, silver-piped for generals and white-piped for others, with velvet bands and silver cap cords for officers, and cloth bands and leather chin straps for lower ranks. As with the képi, a 1929-pattern eagle was worn above a Prussian-style death's head on the cap. Several minor variants of the black uniform were produced during 1933, but the whole outfit was formalized by mid-1934 when the new SS-style Totenkopf with lower jaw was introduced.

During the remaineder of the 1930s, the black service uniform was developed as the SS organization expanded. Greatcoats were produced and a series of specialist arm diamonds or *Ärmelraute* devised for wear on the lower left sleeve. On 21 June 1936, a new and larger SS metal cap eagle replaced the old 1929 pattern, and white shirts were authorized for wear under the black tunic on ceremonial occasions. For evening functions such as parties, dances and so on there were black mess jackets for officers and white 'monkey suits' for waiters, all sporting full SS insignia. Finally, as from 27 June 1939, officers were provided with an all-white version of the service uniform for walking out during the summer period, officially defined as running from 1 April to 30 September each year.

Full-time SS men were regularly issued with items of uniform and equipment. So far as part-timers were concerned, however, all uniform articles had to be purchased by the SS members themselves at their own expense. The following small selection of prices is taken from the extensive Allgemeine-SS Price List of January 1938, and gives a general idea of the cost of items:

Item	Price in Reichsmarks
Black service tunic	34.80
Black breeches	18.00
Black overcoat	45.40
Peaked cap for lower ranks	4.90
Peaked cap for officers	7.50
Peaked cap for generals	7.80
Brown shirt	5.50
Pair marching boots	23.70
1933-pattern dagger	7.10
1936 chained dagger	12.15
Belt buckle for lower ranks	0.50
Belt buckle for officers	1.25
Shoulder strap	0.33
Collar patch	0.60
Swastika armband	0.80
Cuff title	0.75
Honor Chevron of the Old Guard	0.10
Eagle for peaked cap	0.25
Death's head for peaked cap	0.10
Vehicle pennant	1.20

The gradual introduction of the gray service uniform, combined with the sudden reduction in the number of active part-time Allgemeine-SS men because of enhanced conscription at the outbreak of war, led to a surplus of black uniforms building up in SS stores after 1939. Most of these were ultimately stripped of insignia and shipped out for use by native police auxiliaries in the east and the Germanic-SS in the west. Consequently, very few black Allgemeine-SS tunics survived the war with their original German insignia intact.

ABOVE LEFT: Hitler greeting SS-Obergruppenführer Richard Walther Darré, Chef RuSHA, in 1934.

ABOVE: Black service dress was retained for ceremonial use until the outbreak of war. The officer's brocade belt and parade aiguillettes are shown to good effect on this uniform as worn by an Obersturmführer of the SS-VT Standarte 'Der Führer' in 1939.

LEFT: Hitler's rostrum for the Day of German Art parade in Munich in 1939 was fronted by veteran members of the local SS Stammabteilung, distinguished by their silver-gray collar patches.

OPPOSITE TOP: Heydrich's Waffen-SS guards at Prague Castle, spring 1942.

RIGHT: Waffen-SS NCO's 1938-pattern field cap, with the 1940 BEVO-woven insignia.

The Gray Uniform

In 1938 the Allgemeine-SS introduced a very elegant pale gray uniform for its full-time staff, thus bringing the whole SS organization into line with the general war footing of the other uniformed services. The new outfit was identical in style to the black uniform, but bore an SS-pattern shoulder strap on the left shoulder as well as one on the right and replaced the swastika armband with a cloth version of the SS eagle. The idea was to give the appearance of a military rather than political uniform, thus lending some authority to permanent Allgemeine-SS officers who were, by the nature of their employment, exempt from service in the Wehrmacht.

The gray uniform was issued first to headquarters personnel and thereafter to others qualified to wear it. During the war, it was gradually superseded by the Waffen-SS field-gray version, particularly favored by those stationed in the occupied territories. The 40,000 or so active part-time members of the Allgemeine-SS, who were almost exclusively engaged in reserve occupations, were never issued with gray outfits and so continued to wear the black uniform while on duty in Germany. However, by 1945 that most impressive of all SS uniforms, which had been such a status symbol in the prewar days, had become an object of derision since its wearers were increasingly thought of as shirking military service.

LEFT: This very plain and non-regulation 'Litewka' tunic, based on Latvian and Polish designs, was a favorite of SS-Obergruppenführer Oswald Pohl, who wore it on many occasions while carrying out his duties as chief of the WVHA. The Litewka is also known to have been used by the Reich Minister of Food, SS-Obergruppenführer Herbert Backe.

RIGHT: Pohl's regulation pale-gray Allgemeine-SS tunic, with its elegant lines and the distinctive cuff title of a departmental head. Pohl served as an administrator with the imperial navy during World War I, and was later recruited by Himmler to develop the economic and administrative side of the SS and police. Unfortunately, this ultimately involved him in sanctioning the use of slave labor and the leasing of concentration-camp inmates to industrial firms, for which he was condemned to death and hanged in 1951.

Ranks and Titles

Although the SS became one of the most complex of all the Nazi paramilitary organizations, its rank structure remained relatively stable and underwent few major alterations. The definitive SS rank system, dating from April 1942 and lasting until the end of the war, was as follows:

Mannschaften (Other Ranks)
SS-Bewerber – Candidate
SS-Anwärter – Cadet
SS-Mann (SS-Schütze for Waffen-SS) – Private
SS-Oberschütze (Waffen-SS) – Private
   (after 6 months' service)
SS-Sturmmann – Lance Corporal
SS-Rottenführer – Senior Lance Corporal

Unterführer (NCOs)
SS-Unterscharführer – Corporal
SS-Scharführer – Sergeant
SS-Oberscharführer – Staff Sergeant
SS-Hauptscharführer – Sergeant-Major
SS-Sturmscharführer (Waffen-SS) – Company
   Sergeant-Major

(In the Waffen-SS, men holding any of the above five Unterführer ranks could be appointed to serve as their unit's SS-Stabsscharführer or Duty NCO, who fulfilled various administrative, disciplinary and reporting

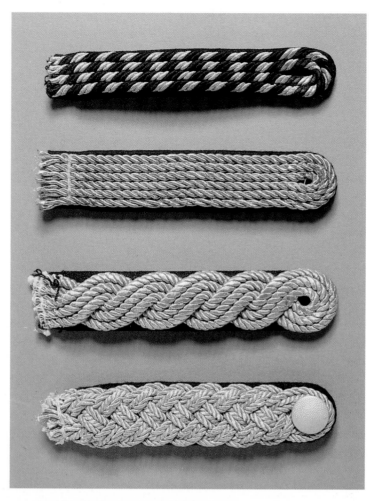

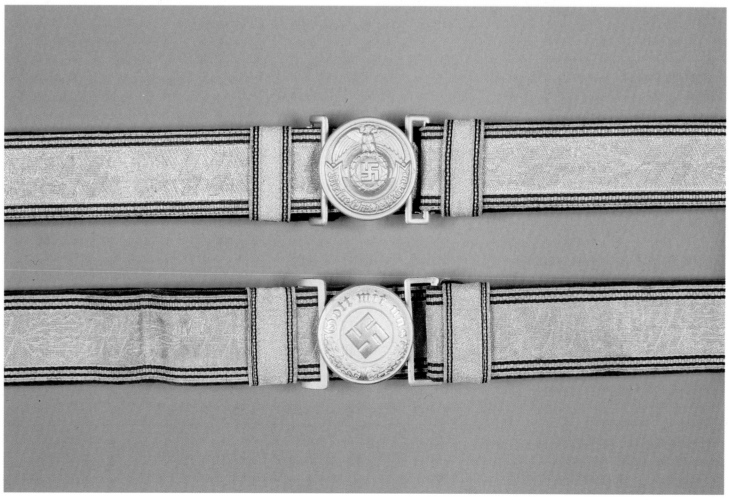

ABOVE LEFT: The four standard Allgemeine-SS shoulder straps, which denoted rank level rather than actual rank. These were worn by, from left to right: enlisted men/NCOs, junior officers, intermediate officers, and senior officers.

LEFT: The SS officer's brocade belt, embroidered with runes and oakleaves, was worn on ceremonial occasions. It is shown here with the SS officer's buckle (above) and the police officer's buckle (below).

ABOVE: A selection of insignia worn by SS general officers.

ABOVE RIGHT: The circular belt buckle for SS officers, and the rectangular buckle for NCOs and other ranks.

RIGHT: SS-Standartenführer Hugo-Gottfried Kraas receiving the Oakleaves to the Knight's Cross from Hitler on 24 January 1944. The officer in the center, Otto Günsche, was later responsible for burning Hitler's body after his suicide.

LEFT: During Mussolini's state visit to Berlin in 1938, his route was lined by soldiers of the SS-VT Standarte 'Deutschland', wearing field-gray rather than black.

RIGHT: Wherever Hitler went, even when meeting children, his SS guards were sure to follow. On 14 June 1938 the Führer strolled through Berlin's Kinder Platz in the company of Brandt, von Below, Goebbels, Wolff, Himmler, Albert Bormann (Martin's brother) and Esser, surrounded by officers and men of the Leibstandarte.

BELOW RIGHT: Troops of the SS Sonderkommando Zossen enjoying a break from their rigorous training at Essenfassen, summer 1933. All wear black 'Krätzchen' field caps and the gray cotton-drill fatigue uniform.

functions. The Stabsscharführer was nicknamed '*der Spiess*' or 'the spear', a traditional term dating back to pikemen of the Middle Ages, and wore two distinctive bands of aluminum *Tresse* around the cuffs.)

Untere Führer (Junior/Company Officers)
SS-Untersturmführer – 2nd Lieutenant
SS-Obersturmführer – Lieutenant
SS-Hauptsturmführer – Captain

Mittlere Führer (Intermediate/Field Officers)
SS-Sturmbannführer – Major
SS-Obersturmbannführer – Lieutenant-Colonel
SS-Standartenführer – Colonel
SS-Oberführer – Senior Colonel

Höhere Führer (Senior/General Officers)
SS-Brigadeführer – Brigadier-General
SS-Gruppenführer – Major-General
SS-Obergruppenführer – Lieutenant-General
SS-Oberst-Gruppenführer – General

(All Waffen-SS generals were awarded their corresponding army rank titles in 1940, e.g. 'SS-Obergruppenführer und General der Waffen-SS'. From 1943, as part of the SS-Police assimilation process, police generals were allowed to incorporate 'Waffen-SS' into their titles, e.g. 'SS-Obergruppenführer und General der Waffen-SS und Polizei'. The same all-embracing titles were extended in 1944 to the HSSPfs (Höhere SS-und Polizeiführer), Himmler's nominees who were technically responsible for all Allgemeine-SS, Waffen-SS and police formations based in their territories.)

Himmler retained his overall authority as Reichsführer-SS. As with the SA, NSKK, HJ and all other NSDAP formations, Hitler himself was ultimately Commander-in-Chief of the SS and held the personal title of 'Der Oberste Führer der Schutzstaffel'.

Allgemeine-SS ranks took precedence over those of the Waffen-SS and police in official SS correspondence. Allgemeine-SS officers and NCOs who joined the Waffen-SS during the war retained their Allgemeine-SS ranks and had them automatically upgraded if they were promoted to higher levels in the Waffen-SS.

Waffen-SS officer candidates or Führerbewerber (FB) had to serve as NCOs before being commissioned. During an 18-month period, the officer cadet or Führeranwärter (FA) rose through the grades of SS-Junker, SS-Standartenjunker and SS-Standartenoberjunker, which equated to SS-Unterscharführer, SS-Scharführer and SS-Hauptscharführer respectively. Reserve officers who intended to serve only for the duration of the war were known as RFB, RFA, SS-Junker der Reserve and so on. A similar scheme existed for potential NCOs. Civilian specialists such as interpreters and doctors employed by the Waffen-SS were known as Sonderführer or Fachführer, and were distinguished by (S) or (F) after their ranks.

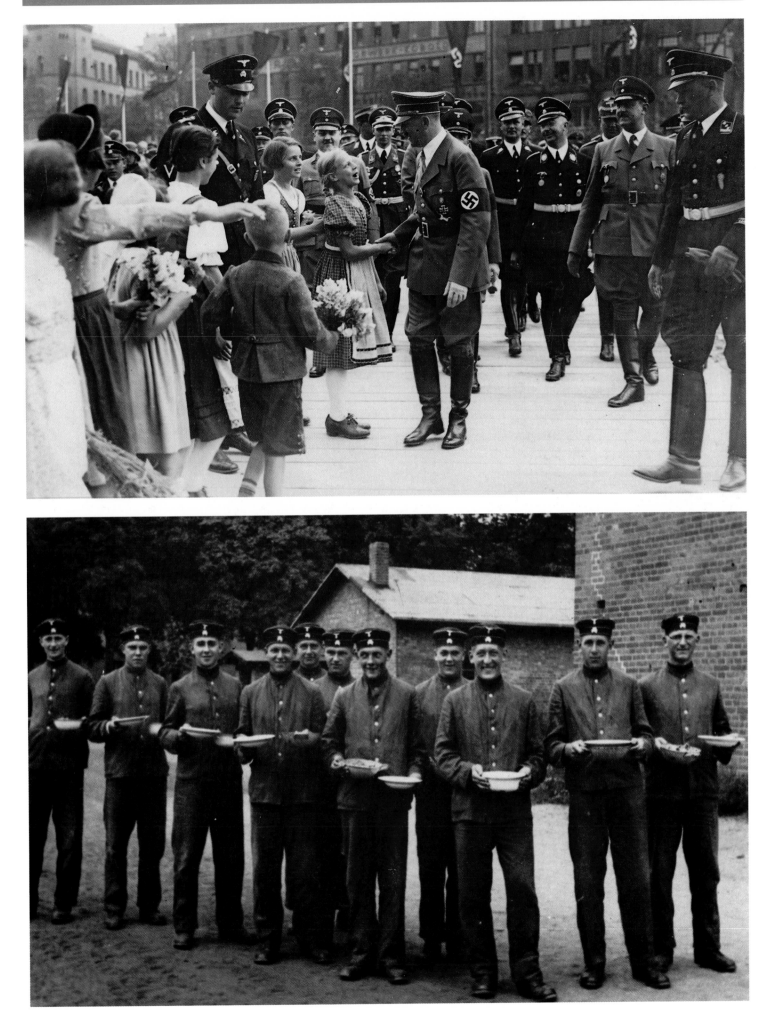

Daggers

The SS dagger, or 'Dienstdolch', was introduced with its SA counterpart on 15 December 1933. Black and silver in color, it bore the SS motto on the blade, and runes and an eagle on the grip. Its general design was based on that of a seventeenth-century German hunting knife known as the 'Holbein', which had a representation of Holbein's painting *The Dance of Death* on its scabbard. Worn by all ranks of the Allgemeine-SS with service and walking-out dress, the SS dagger was presented to its owner only at the special 9 November ceremony when he graduated from SS-Anwärter to SS-Mann. It was not issued at any other time, or en masse like the daggers of the more plebian SA. Each SS member paid the full cost of his dagger, usually in small instalments, prior to its presentation.

In February 1934 the private purchase or 'trading-in' of SS daggers on the open market was forbidden. Thereafter, daggers could only be ordered from manufacturers through SS headquarters, for issue via the three main SS uniform distribution centers at Munich, Dresden and Berlin. Moreover, it was made a disciplinary offense for an SS man to dispose of or lose his dagger, on the grounds that it was a symbol of his office. In that way, it was assured that no unauthorized person could buy or otherwise acquire an SS dagger. As of 25 January 1935, members dismissed from the SS had to surrender their daggers, even though they were personal property paid for by their own means. In cases of voluntary resignation or normal retirement, however, daggers could be retained, and the person in question was given a certificate stating that he was entitled to possess it.

Only the finest makers of edged weapons were contracted to produce the 1933-pattern SS dagger. These included Böker & Co., Carl Eickhorn, Gottlieb Hammesfahr, Richard Herder, Jacobs & Co., Robert Klaas, Ernst Pack & Söhne, and C. Bertram Reinhardt. The earliest pieces from the 1933-35 period featured the maker's trademark on the blade, a dark blue-black anodyzed steel scabbard, and nickel-silver fittings with the crossguard reverse stamped 'I', 'II', or 'III' to denote that the dagger had passed inspection at the main SS uniform-distribution center responsible for issuing it, viz. Munich, Dresden or Berlin, respectively. During 1936-37, makers' marks were replaced by RZM code numbers (e.g. RZM M7/66 for Eickhorn), scabbards began to be finished with black paint, and the stamped inspection numerals were discontinued as the RZM had by then entirely taken over the regulation of quality control. Finally, from 1938, nickel-silver gave way to cheaper plated steel for the mounts and aluminum for the grip eagle. Yet, despite the lowering standard of materials used, a high-quality appearance was always maintained and the daggers were consistent in their fine finish. In September 1940, due to national economies, the 1933-pattern dagger was withdrawn from production for the duration of the war.

The SS dagger was suspended at an angle from a single leather strap until November 1934, when Himmler introduced a vertical hanger for wear with service

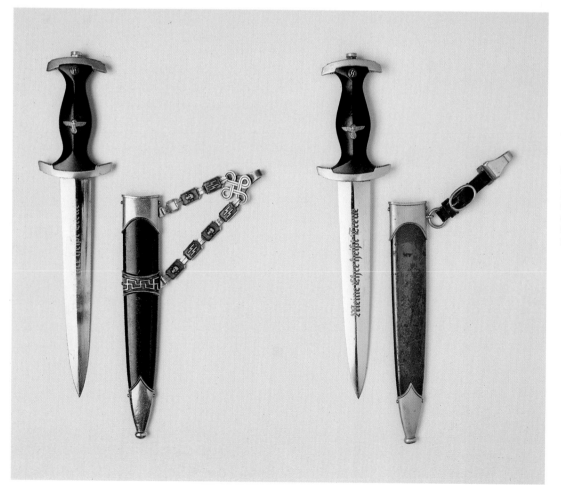

LEFT: The 1936-pattern SS chained dagger (left) and the 1933-pattern dagger with hanging strap.

RIGHT: On Labor Day in 1935, the Führer reviewed a marchpast of the Hitler Youth in Berlin's Lustgarten. On his right, with dagger clearly worn, is SS-Gruppenführer Philipp Bouhler, head of Hitler's secretariat or private Chancellery. While Bouhler and Goebbels wear the 'Tag der Arbeit 1935' day badge specially produced for the event, Hitler does not. The Führer preferred to use as few uniform adornments as possible and, surprisingly, did not even consent to wearing his Golden Party Badge until 1936.

dress during crowd control. However, the vertical hanger, while more stable, was too reminiscent of the humble bayonet frog, and in 1936 the single strap was reintroduced for both the walking-out and service uniforms. Thereafter, the vertical hanger was restricted to use on route marches and military exercises.

A more ornate SS dagger, to be worn only by officers and by those Old Guard NCOs and other ranks who had joined the organization prior to 30 January 1933, was introduced by Himmler on 21 June 1936. Generally known as the 'chained dagger', it was very similar to the 1933 pattern but was suspended by means of linked octagonal plates, ornately embossed with death's heads and SS runes, and featured a central scabbard mount decorated with swastikas. During the 1936-37 period these chains and fittings, which were designed by Karl Diebitsch, were made from nickel-silver. Later examples were in nickel-plated steel with slightly smaller, less oval-shaped skulls. Chained daggers bore no makers' marks and it is likely that only one firm, probably Carl Eickhorn, which featured the chained dagger in its sales catalog, was contracted to produce them. Each chained dagger had to be privately purchased through SS headquarters.

In the spring of 1940, SS-Obergruppenführer Fritz Weitzel suggested to Himmler that an army-type dagger should be introduced for wear exclusively by officers of the Waffen-SS, who had performed so well in the opening stages of the war but were prevented by regulations from wearing the Allgemeine-SS dagger with their field-gray uniform. However, Himmler rejected the idea out of hand. It was not until 15 February 1943, during the preparations for the SS assault on Kharkov, that Waffen-SS officers were finally permitted to wear the chained dagger with their field-gray walking-out dress. As a concession to their military status, they were also given the right to use an army-pattern porte-

pee knot, tied about the grip and crossguard in a new and unique SS style. Four months later, wear of the chained dagger and knot with field-gray uniform was extended to officers of the security police and SD, and thus the latter became the only branch of the Allgemeine-SS whose members were permitted to sport dagger knots.

Production of the chained dagger had to be discontinued at the end of 1943 because of material shortages, and its wear was subsequently forbidden for the duration of the war.

In addition to the standard 1933-pattern and 1936-pattern SS daggers, several special presentation variants were also produced. The first of these was the so-called Röhm SS Honor Dagger, 9900 of which were distributed in February 1934 by SA Stabschef Ernst Röhm to members of the SS Old Guard. It took the form of a basic 1933-pattern dagger with the addition of the dedication 'In herzlicher Kameradschaft, Ernst Röhm' ('In heartfelt comradeship, Ernst Röhm') etched on the reverse side of the blade. Following the Night of the Long Knives, 200 similar daggers etched 'In herzlicher Kameradschaft, H. Himmler', were presented by the Reichsführer to SS personnel who had participated in the bloody purge of the SA. A very ornate and expensive SS honor dagger, with oakleaf-decorated crossguards, leather-covered scabbard and damascus steel blade, was instituted by Himmler in 1936 for award to high-ranking officers in recognition of special achievement. When one was presented to the NSDAP Treasurer Franz Xaver Schwarz, who was also an SS-Oberst-Gruppenführer and second only to Himmler on the SS seniority list, he responded by secretly commissioning the Eickhorn firm to produce an even more elaborate example, with fittings and chain hanger in solid silver, which he then gave to the Reichsführer as a birthday present.

Swords

During the 1933-36 era, SS officers and NCOs engaged in ceremonial duties were permitted to wear a variety of privately-purchased army-pattern sabers, often with silver rather than regulation gilt fittings. In 1936, however, at the same time as the introduction of the chained dagger, a series of standardized swords in the classic straight-bladed *'Degen'* style was created specifically for members of the SS and police, emphasizing the close relationship between the two organizations. There were minor differences between degen for officers and those for NCOs, while SS swords featured runes on the grip, and police examples the police eagle. Personnel attached to SS Reiterstandarten retained the traditional curved saber for use on horseback.

SS NCOs could readily purchase their swords, via local units, from the SS administrative department in Berlin. The officer's sword, on the other hand, which was referred to as the *Ehrendegen des Reichsführers-SS*, or Reichsführer's Sword of Honor, was given an elevated status and could not be worn automatically by every SS officer. It was bestowed by Himmler only upon selected Allgemeine-SS commanders and all graduates

ABOVE LEFT: On 30 August 1934, Hitler visited the site in Munich where the new Brown House, or NSDAP headquarters, was being built. He was accompanied by his chief SS and SA adjutants, Julius Schaub and Wilhelm Brückner, and also by Baldur von Schirach, leader of the Hitler Youth.

RIGHT: The Reichsführer's Sword of Honor, bestowed by Himmler on selected SS officers.

FAR RIGHT: SS sword knots worn by officers (left) and junior NCOs (right).

of the Waffen-SS Junkerschulen at Bad Tölz and Braunschweig. Each presentation of the Ehrendegen was accompanied by a citation in which the Reichsführer instructed the recipient: 'I award you the SS sword. Never draw it without reason, or sheathe it without honor!' ('Ich verleihe Ihnen den Degen der SS. Ziehen Sie ihn niemals ohne Not! Stecken Sie ihn niemals ein ohne Ehre!') However, despite Himmler's dramatic exhortations, the sword never became a cult weapon to the same extent as the revered SS dagger. Manufacture ceased on 25 January 1941 for the duration of the war, and SS officers commissioned after that date frequently reverted to the old practice of carrying army sabers.

Still more exclusive were the so-called *Geburtstagsdegen* or birthday swords, given by Himmler to SS generals and other leading Nazi personalities as birth-day presents. They were made to order by Germany's master swordsmith, Paul Müller, who was director of the SS damascus school at Dachau. The Geburtstagsdegen featured hallmarked silver fittings and blades of the finest damascus steel with exquisitely raised and gilded personal dedications from Himmler. The sword given to von Ribbentrop on his birthday in 1939, for example, bore the golden legend 'Meinem lieben Joachim von Ribbentrop zum 30.4.39 – H. Himmler, Reichsführer-SS' ('To my dear friend Joachim von Ribbentrop on 30 April 1939 – H. Himmler, Reichsführer-SS') set between two swastikas. Hitler received a similar weapon, the blade inscription of which read, 'In good times and bad, we will always remain steadfast', thereby extolling the virtues and loyalty of the SS, and binding its member directly to him.

The SS Death's Head Ring

One of the most obscure yet most potent of all SS uniform accouterments was the *Totenkopfring der SS*, or SS Death's Head Ring, instituted by Himmler on 10 April 1934. The Totenkopfring was not classed as a national decoration as it was in the gift of the Reichsführer. However, it ranked as a senior award within the SS brotherhood, recognizing the wearer's personal achievement, devotion to duty, and loyalty to the Führer and his ideals.

The concept and runic form of the ring was undoubtedly adopted by Himmler from pagan German mythology, which related how Thor possessed a pure silver ring on which people could take oaths (much as Christians swear on the Bible), and how binding treaties were carved in runes on Wotan's spear. The Death's Head Ring comprised a massive band of oakleaves deeply embossed with a Totenkopf and a number of symbolic runes. Each piece was cast and hand-finished by specially commissioned jewelers working for the firm of Otto Gahr in Munich, and was finely engraved inside the band with the letters 'S.lb' (the abbreviation for 'Seinem lieben' or, roughly, 'To Dear') followed by the recipient's surname, the date of presentation and a facsimile of Himmler's signature.

Initially, the weighty silver ring was reserved primarily for those Old Guard veterans with SS membership numbers below 5000 but qualifications for the award were gradually extended until, by 1939, virtually all officers with over three years' service were eligible. Award of the ring could be postponed if the prospective holder had been punished for contravention of the SS discipline code. Each ring was presented with a citation which read:

'I award you the SS Death's Head Ring. The ring symbolizes our loyalty to the Führer, our steadfast obedience and our brotherhood and comradeship. The Death's Head reminds us that we should be ready at any time to lay down our lives for the good of the Germanic people. The runes diametrically opposite the Death's Head are symbols from our past of the prosperity which we will restore through National Socialism. The two Sig-Runes stand for the name of our SS. The swastika and the Hagall-Rune represent our unshakable faith in the ultimate victory of our philosophy. The ring is wreathed in oak, the traditional German leaf. The Death's Head Ring cannot be bought or sold and must never fall into the hands of those not entitled to wear it. When you leave the SS, or when you die, the ring must be returned to the Reichsführer-SS. The unauthorized acquisition of duplicates of the ring is forbidden and punishable by law. Wear the ring with honor!'

H. HIMMLER

The ring, which was to be worn only on the ring finger of the left hand, was bestowed on set SS promotion dates. All awards were recorded in the Dienstaltersliste, or Officers' Seniority List, and the personnel files of the holders. All ring-holders who were demoted, suspended or dismissed from the SS, or who resigned or retired, had to return their rings and citations to the SS Personalhauptamt. Those later accepted back into the organization would again qualify for the ring. When a serving ring-holder died, his relatives could retain his

LEFT: Hitler being followed by the Leibstandarte guard of honor commanded by Hauptsturmführer Theodor Wisch, February 1938.

RIGHT: Police NCO's sword with SS knot, as worn by police warrant officers who held SS membership.

citation as a keepsake, but had to return his ring to the SS Personalhauptamt which arranged for its preservation in Himmler's castle at Wewelsburg in permanent commemoration of the holder. Similarly, if a ringholder fighting with the Wehrmacht or Waffen-SS was killed in action, his ring had to be retrieved from the body by members of his unit and returned by the unit commander to the SS Personalhauptamt for preservation. In effect, the returned rings of dead SS men constituted military memorials and were cared for as such at Wewelsburg's ever-growing *Schrein des Inhabers des Totenkopfringes* or Shrine to Holders of the Death's Head Ring.

The Death's Head Ring became so sought-after an honor that many SS and police men not entitled to wear it had a variety of unofficial 'skull rings' produced in gold and silver by local jewelers and even concentration-camp inmates. However, these lacked any runic symbolism and were rather vulgar representations of the real thing.

On 17 October 1944, the Reichsführer-SS canceled further manufacture and presentation of the Totenkopfring for the duration of the war. In the spring of 1945, on Himmler's orders, all the rings which had been kept in the shrine were blast-sealed into a mountainside near Wewelsburg, to prevent their capture by the Allies. To this day, they have never been found.

Between 1934 and 1944, around 14,500 rings were awarded. As at 1 January 1945, according to official SS statistics, 64 per cent of these had been returned on the deaths of their holders (i.e. those rings to be buried at Wewelsburg), 10 per cent had been lost on the battlefield, and 26 per cent were either still in the possession of ring holders or otherwise unaccounted for. That would mean that, in theory, about 3500 rings might have been in circulation at the end of the war. The history of the SS Death's Head Ring indicates the gravity with which the SS treated their regalia.

Flags and Banners

From 4 July 1926, the SS had the distinction of keeping the most revered flag in the Third Reich, the *Blutfahne*, or Blood Banner, which had been carried at the head of the Nazi Old Guard during the Munich Putsch when they were fired upon by the police. It was spattered with the gore of those shot during the encounter and was thereafter considered to be something of a holy relic. SS man Jakob Grimminger of the Munich SS detachment, a veteran of the World War I Gallipoli Campaign and

TOP: The SS Death's Head Ring. This one was awarded to SS-Hauptsturmführer Kurt Taschner in 1942.

LEFT: These plates from the 1943 edition of the *Organisationsbuch der NSDAP* illustrate a selection of SS standards and uniform styles. Note the 1940-pattern Feldzeichen of the Leibstandarte-SS 'Adolf Hitler'.

RIGHT: The Sturmbannfahne of the 14th SS Signals Battalion (Vienna). Of particular interest are the standard-bearer's gorget and bandolier.

participant in the 1922 'Battle of Coburg' when the SA had routed the local Communists, was accorded the honor of being appointed the first official bearer of the Blood Banner and he retained that position throughout his career. The last public appearance of the Blutfahne was at the funeral of Adolf Wagner, Gauleiter of Munich-Upper Bavaria, in April 1944. By that time, Grimminger had attained the rank of SS-Standarten-führer, his association with the mystical flag having assured him a steady succession of promotions.

Every Allgemeine-SS Standarte was represented by a banner or *Feldzeichen*, which was itself known as the regimental 'Standarte'. Somewhat reminiscent of the ancient Roman vexillum banner, it took the form of a wooden pole surmounted by a metal eagle and wreathed swastika, below which was a black and silver boxed nameplate bearing the title or area of the SS Standarte on the front and the initials 'NSDAP' on the back. From the box was suspended a red silk flag with a black static swastika on a white circle. The motto 'Deutschland

Erwache' ('Germany Awake') was embroidered in bullion on the obverse, with 'Nat. Soz. Deutsche Arbeiterpartei – Sturmabteilung' on the reverse. The whole item was finished off with a black/white/red fringe and tassels. Apart from the black name box, the SS Feldzeichen was identical to that of the SA.

When an SS unit achieved roughly regimental proportions, it was awarded a Feldzeichen in a mass pseudo-religious ceremony which took place each September as part of the annual NSDAP celebrations at Nürnberg. During the proceedings, Hitler would present many new standards to regimental commanders and touch them with the Blutfahne which Grimminger was carrying alongside, so linking in spirit the most recent SS members with the martyrs of the Munich Putsch.

SS Reiterstandarten carried similar but distinctive Feldzeichen which had the 'Deutschland Erwache' flag hanging from a wooden bar fixed at right angles to the standard pole. In place of the name box, these cavalry

LEFT: Hitler consecrated over 200 new SA and SS standards at the Reichsparteitag in 1934, closely attended by Jakob Grimminger, carrying the Blutfahne.

RIGHT: A reconstruction of the pre-1940 Feldzeichen carried by the Leibstandarte-SS 'Adolf Hitler'. The original standard top used by the Führer's guard still lies in a Moscow museum, having been captured by the Red Army in 1945. The Leibstandarte's distinctive white-leather parade equipment was introduced in 1936, and was unique to that regiment.

Adolf Hitler

DEUTSCHLAND

ERWACHE

ABOVE: An SS vehicle pennant with its foul-weather cover. This item was authorized for use by all SS junior officers on their staff cars. When the officer concerned left his vehicle, regulations dictated that the pennant be removed.

LEFT: Waffen-SS men could purchase photograph albums like this from their unit's canteen shop.

ABOVE RIGHT: The distinctive accouterments of an SS standard-bearer – gorget, bandolier and gauntlets.

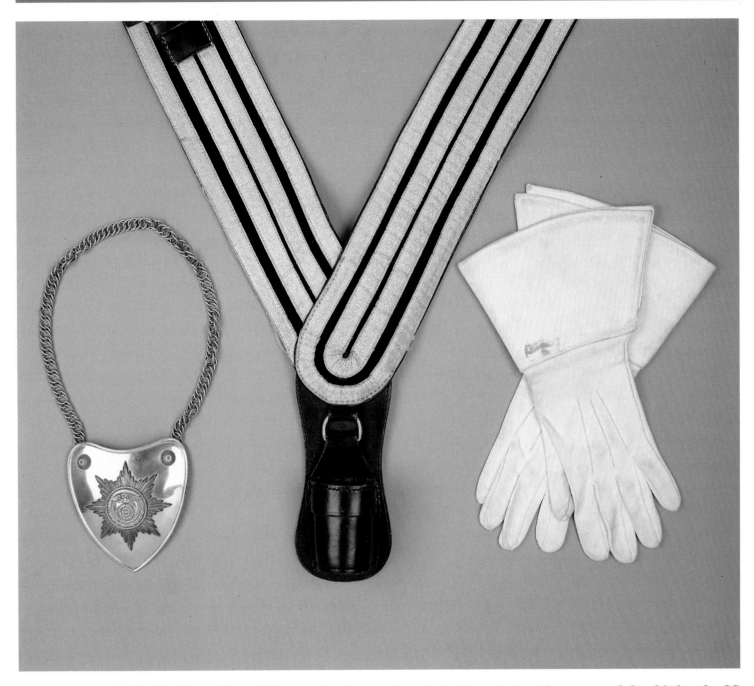

standards featured a black patch, or *Fahnenspiegel*, on the flag cloth, bearing crossed lances and the unit designation in silver.

Each SS Sturmbann was represented by a *Sturmbannfahne* or battalion flag, which took the form of a red ground with a large black mobile swastika on a white circular field, with black and silver twisted cord edging. In the upper left corner, or canton, a black Fahnenspiegel was embroidered in silver thread with the Sturmbann and Standarte numbers in Roman and Arabic numerals respectively. The majority of these SS flags were made by the firm of Fahnen-Hoffmann, Berlin.

SS standard-bearers initially wore a heart-shaped SA-style metal gorget or Kornet, dating from 1929, upon which was affixed a gilded eight-pointed sunburst surmounted by a facsimile of the centerpiece of the SA belt buckle. In 1938, a new and unique SS-pattern standard-bearer's gorget appeared, crescent-shaped and featuring a large eagle and swastika and a suspen-

sion chain decorated with runes and death's heads. SS flag-bearers also wore a massive bandolier in black, with silver brocade edging.

Command flags, or *Kommandoflaggen*, in the shape of rigid pennants on flag poles, were carried as unit markers at large parades or, in smaller versions, were flown from the fenders of staff cars and other official vehicles. They were square, rectangular or triangular in form depending upon designation, and were made of black-and-white waterproof cloth with rustproof silver thread. Command flags were usually covered in a transparent Celluloid casing during inclement weather. Each SS headquarters was required to keep on hand one official vehicle flag and one command pennant for the Reichsführer-SS, for use in the event of a 'flying visit' by Himmler. Other Kommandoflaggen included those for the heads of the SS Hauptämter, SS Oberabschnitte and Abschnitte commanders, the leaders of Standarten, Reiterstandarten, Sturmbanne, SS stores and Inspectorates, and senior Sponsoring Members.

THE WAFFEN-SS

When Hitler assumed the Chancellorship, he felt that he could not entirely rely on the traditional Reichswehr guards appointed by the State to protect him. Consequently, he quickly issued instructions for the formation of a new full-time armed SS unit whose sole function would be to escort him at all times, whether in Berlin or on his official journeys throughout Germany. At the Party Day Rally in September 1933, the detachment was officially named the Leibstandarte-SS 'Adolf Hitler' or LAH, which may best be translated as the 'Adolf Hitler' Life Guards, invoking memories of the Bavarian royal bodyguard regiments. Under Sepp Dietrich, the Leibstandarte came to be in exclusive prominence around Hitler, its men serving not only as his guards but also as his adjutants, drivers, servants and waiters.

At the same time as the infant Leibstandarte was being nurtured, other small groups of armed SS men were set up all over Germany to be at the disposal of local Nazi leaders. As a general rule, each SS Abschnitt recruited its own *Kasernierte Hundertschaft* of 100 or so barracked troops, and several of these were amalgamated in key areas to become company- or even battalion-sized *Politische Bereitschaften*, or PBs, political reserve squads. Along with the Leibstandarte, the PBs played a significant part in the Night of the Long Knives, as a result of which they were expanded into a new force known as the SS-Verfügungstruppe or SS-VT, under Paul Hausser.

Meanwhile, a third armed SS formation known as the *Wachverbände* had been created specifically for the purpose of guarding the growing number of concentration-camp inmates. Commanded by Theodor Eicke, this formation grew to incorporate five battalions which in March 1936 were named the SS-Totenkopfverbände or SS-TV (SS Death's Head Units) because of their distinctive collar patches. That same month, the Leibstandarte played a leading role in Hitler's first move outwards when it provided the advance guard in the reoccupation of the Rhineland.

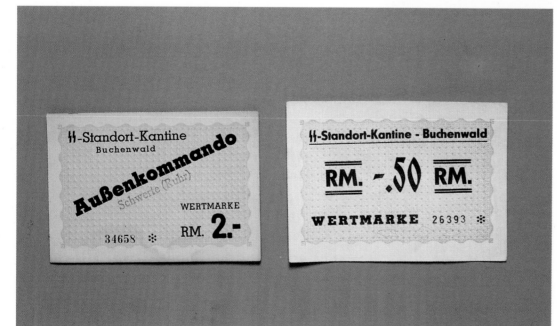

PREVIOUS PAGES: The entire Leibstandarte marched past its Führer as Hess, Dietrich and Himmler looked on, 30 January 1938.

ABOVE: SS-Obergruppenführer Theodor Eicke wearing the Knight's Cross with Oakleaves.

LEFT: Concentration-camp guards received a percentage of their wages in the form of 'garrison tokens', which could be used to buy food and sundry items from the camp canteen and shop.

RIGHT: Heinrich Hoffmann, Hitler's personal photographer, with Sepp Dietrich at Berchtesgaden during the summer of 1944.

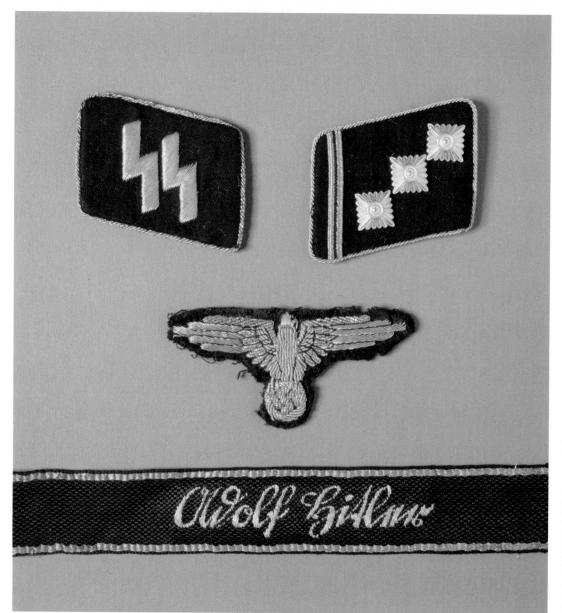

LEFT: Collar patches, arm eagle and cuff title as worn by an Obersturmführer of the Leibstandarte-SS 'Adolf Hitler'.

BELOW: On 6 August 1944, Oberst-Gruppenführer Dietrich became the sixteenth recipient of the Diamonds to the Knight's Cross. The presentation photograph was skillfully taken so as to conceal the injury to Hitler's right arm, which had been sustained during the bomb-plot assassination attempt a fortnight earlier.

RIGHT: The Leibstandarte in the Berlin victory parade on 19 July 1940. The high-quality officer's tunic, on the left, contrasts sharply with the field blouses worn by the NCOs and men.

BELOW RIGHT: Theodor Wisch, shown here at the left during the 9 November 1935 celebrations in Munich, was one of the original 120 members of the Leibstandarte and led the LAH Division during the Normandy battles of June-August 1944. He was badly wounded on 20 August and spent the rest of the war on attachment to the SS Führungshauptamt.

During the rest of the prewar period, the armed SS developed under the direction of innovative officers who favored the tactics of assault detachments, shock troops and mobile battle groups. Soon even the Wehrmacht's eyebrows rose as SS troops on maneuvers covered almost two miles in 20 minutes in full battle order. By September 1939, the Leibstandarte had expanded to include three motorized infantry battalions and ancillary units, while the SS-VT comprised the 'Deutschland', 'Germania' and 'Der Führer' Standarten with artillery support. The Death's Head Units were even more numerous, with five Totenkopfstandarten and a Home Guard battalion, the so-called SS-Heimwehr, in Danzig.

So why had there been such a rapid militarization of large sections of the SS? The reason was a simple one. The SS was primarily a civil police force which Hitler hoped would eventually maintain order not only in Germany but throughout Nazi-occupied Europe. To do so, however, it would first have to win its spurs on the battlefield. It would be necessary for the SS and police, in their own closed units, to prove themselves at the front and make blood sacrifices to the same degree as

any other branch of the armed forces. Only then could the SS possess the authority necessary for its future role in the New Order.

The Leibstandarte, 'Deutschland', 'Germania' and the SS-Heimwehr Danzig all participated actively in the conquest of Poland. At the end of 1939, the term 'Waffen-SS' began to be used when referring to the armed SS formations, which Hausser successfully argued needed to be organized into full divisions to operate efficiently. Within a few months the three SS-VT regiments had been merged into the first full SS division, the SS-Verfügungsdivision or SS-V, and the SS-Totenkopfstandarten united to become the SS-Totenkopf-Division or SS-T. A third combat division, the so-called Polizei-Division, was created almost overnight by a mass transfer of uniformed police personnel into the Waffen-SS. The Blitzkrieg across Holland, Belgium and France during May-June 1940 established beyond doubt the fighting reputation of the Waffen-SS, with six of their number winning the coveted Knight's Cross.

Germany's success in western Europe opened up a new reservoir of pro-Nazi foreigners whom the Wehrmacht had no authority to conscript. They were recruited into a new Waffen-SS division named 'Wiking', under Felix Steiner, at the end of 1940. In April 1941, the Leibstandarte and SS-V, the latter having been awarded the title SS-Division 'Reich', raced through Yugoslavia and Greece.

LEFT: This commemorative folder was produced in January 1943 and contained 12 photographic prints by SS war correspondents showing the Leibstandarte in action.

BELOW LEFT: Assault engineers and artillery of the SS-Totenkopf Division crossing La Bassée Canal in northern France, May 1940. Camouflage clothing had not been widely distributed to SS-TV troops at this early stage in the war, and field-gray army-pattern tunics were the order of the day.

RIGHT: Greatcoat of an Obersturmführer of the Totenkopf Division, 1940. During the formation of the first SS field division in the fall of 1939, it was decided that its personnel should receive matching collar-patches, with ranks being indicated solely by the shoulder straps in army fashion. The matching collar patch order was rescinded the following May, but such insignia continued to be worn well into 1942.

LEFT: Personnel of the Waffen-SS reconnaissance units frequently advanced deep into enemy territory, well ahead of the main Wehrmacht forces.

BELOW LEFT: SS-Totenkopf troops celebrate after the fall of France. The man on the right wears the 'Hilfs-Krankenträger' armband of an auxiliary stretcher-bearer, and a typical mix of clothing and insignia is evident from the appearance of the others.

RIGHT: Engineers of the SS-Polizei-Division building a bridge across the Veilikaya River near Opochka, northern Russia, summer 1943.

BELOW: Gruppenführer Felix Steiner, commander of the SS-Division 'Wiking'.

At dawn on 22 June 1941, Hitler ordered his forces into Russia to begin the epic conflict of ideologies which became a war of extermination and changed forever the hitherto generally chivalrous character of the Waffen-SS. 'Reich' was heavily engaged at Minsk, Smolensk and Borodino, where Hausser lost an eye, and the division came within a few kilometers of Moscow at the end of the year. The force of the Russian counter-offensive during the harsh winter of 1941-42 stunned the Germans, many of whom found themselves cut off in isolated 'pockets', the most notable being that at Demjansk which contained six divisions, including 'Totenkopf'.

During 1942, the SS divisions were refitted with a strong tank component. In May, 'Reich' was renamed 'Das Reich' and in September the SS-Kavallerie-Division was activated for anti-partisan duties behind the lines. December saw the formation of two completely new Waffen-SS divisions, 'Hohenstaufen' and 'Frundsberg', by which time SS troops in the field numbered around 200,000.

The Soviet offensive of December 1942 proved disastrous for the Germans. The Sixth Army was destroyed at Stalingrad and other German forces in the Caucasus also faced the grim possibility of encirclement. However, the Russian thrust had become dangerously over-extended and in March 1943 an SS-Panzer-Korps comprising the Leibstandarte, 'Das Reich' and 'Totenkopf' took Kharkov, a prestige target. For the first time, a substantial body of Waffen-SS troops fought together under their own generals and the result was a resounding victory. To Hitler, who was becoming

increasingly disillusioned with army failures, it was proof of the fighting capabilities of the Waffen-SS. In July, the SS-Panzer-Korps played its part in the mass armored battles around Kursk and again fought well, despite being weakened by the removal of the Leibstandarte which was transferred to Italy to bolster German forces there. The position on the eastern front underwent a drastic deterioration when the Soviets launched an offensive across the Ukraine at the end of the year. The Wiking division was trapped in the Korsun-Cherkassy pocket in a scene reminiscent of Stalingrad, while the Leibstandarte and elements of 'Das Reich' were encircled at Kamenets Podolsky and had to be rescued by 'Hohenstaufen' and 'Frundsberg'. Worn down and exhausted, the Waffen-SS formations were now increasingly unable to stem the advancing Russian tide.

In the spring of 1944 the battered SS divisions were sent westwards and refitted in preparation for the expected Anglo-American invasion. Throughout July, the Leibstandarte, 'Das Reich', 'Hohenstaufen', 'Frundsberg' and the recently mustered 'Hitlerjugend' and 'Götz von Berlichingen' divisions struggled ceaselessly to contain the Allies in their beachhead, but were overtaken by sheer weight of numbers. Simultaneously, the Red Army struck again in the east and ripped the German lines apart. 'Wiking' and 'Totenkopf' repulsed the Soviet attack on Warsaw during August, while in the Balkans the backbone of the German defense was provided by 'Prinz Eugen', 'Handschar' and other nominally second-grade SS formations which had been withdrawn from their usual anti-partisan duties. Increasingly, while ordinary German soldiers were prepared to surrender, it was left to the Waffen-SS to fight

LEFT: A wounded member of the 'Hitlerjugend' Division surrenders near Falaise, August 1944. He is wearing the new camouflage drill tunic on top of a standard field blouse.

BELOW LEFT: The 'Sonderkraft-fahrzeug' series of half-tracks was widely used by the Waffen-SS in a variety of roles. This one, bearing the tactical symbols of HQ Staff, 2nd Battalion, 1st SS-Panzergrenadier Regiment, was on the road to Milan, September 1943.

RIGHT: Soldiers of the SS Cavalry Brigade on anti-partisan patrol in Russia, summer 1942.

BELOW: The floppy battle-worn appearance of the 'crusher' cap made it a popular item of headgear right up until the end of the war. Here it is worn by an NCO of the SS-Panzer-Aufklärungs-Abteilung 1 at Kaiserbarracke in the Ardennes, 17 December 1944. The Schwimmwagen driver wears a civilian leather motoring helmet.

LEFT: One of a series of staged shots showing heavily-laden Waffen-SS troops advancing during the Ardennes offensive.

BELOW: These two young soldiers captured near Bastogne at the end of 1944 epitomize the exhausted state of the Waffen-SS, which was by then almost totally worn out as a result of continual front-line action.

BOTTOM: Wisch, Wünsche, Dietrich and Witt, representing the 1st SS-Panzerkorps, were Hitler's guests at Berchtesgaden in 1944.

RIGHT: Soldiers save what they can from an SS vehicle burning outside the Anhalter station in Berlin, April 1945.

on. In September the British airborne landing at Arnhem was defeated by 'Hohenstaufen' and 'Frundsberg'. This victory, and the general slowing down of the Allied advance across France, persuaded Hitler to launch a major offensive through the Ardennes, spearheaded by Dietrich's Sixth SS-Panzer Army, in an attempt to repeat the successes of 1940. However, the hilly and wooded terrain naturally favored defensive action and the German advance ground to a halt. With a virtual stalemate in the west, Hitler pulled his SS divisions out and sent them eastwards, where the situation had once more became desperate.

At the beginning of 1945, the Soviets swept across Poland. Even so, Hitler's main concern was to safeguard the tenuous hold he still maintained over the Hungarian oilfields. The SS cavalry divisions 'Florian Geyer' and 'Maria Theresa' were besieged in Budapest, and 'Totenkopf' and 'Wiking' failed in efforts to relieve them. The deployment of Sixth SS-Panzer Army reinforced by the 'Reichsführer-SS' division was the last gamble, and it came to nothing. The failure of the Waffen-SS in Hungary had a devastating effect on Hitler, who had come to expect the impossible from them, and he openly accused Dietrich and his subordinates of betrayal. Nevertheless, SS troops carried on fighting as loyally as ever as they slowly retreated into Germany, bowed under the weight of superior Allied numbers and equipment. During the last week in April, a battle group of hard-core Waffen-SS engaged in a life and death struggle to defend the Führerbunker. By that time, most SS units had accepted the reality of the situation and were pushing westwards to surrender to the British and Americans.

It is estimated that some 180,000 Waffen-SS soldiers were killed in action during World War II, with about 400,000 wounded and a further 70,000 listed 'missing'.

These figures are put into their true perspective when it is considered that the entire British army, navy and air force combined suffered a total of 270,000 fatal casualties between 1939 and 1945, and US losses were 300,000. By the closing stages of the war, SS soldiers were normally in their late teens, and the average age of a Waffen-SS junior officer was 20, with a life expectancy of two months at the front.

The loyalty and determination of the Waffen-SS belied the fact that the greater part of its strength, over 57 percent, ultimately comprised non-German nationals. Large numbers of pro-Germans, anti-Bolsheviks, members of local pseudo-Nazi political parties, adventurers and simple opportunists spread right across occupied Europe were only too eager to throw in their lot with the winning side. Flemings, Dutchmen, Italians, Walloons, Norwegians, Danes, Frenchmen, Latvians, Ukrainians, Rumanians, Estonians, Croats and many others, including even a few British, enlisted in the Waffen-SS, often in their own units with their own distinctive insignia. The westerners generally per-

LEFT: Three SS-Hauptsturmführer attached to the 'Handschar' division at the end of 1943. Their decorations indicate that they are German nationals. The officer in the middle, a veteran of the SA/SS rally at Braunschweig (Brunswick) in 1931, wears the blank right-hand collar patch sported by some 'Handschar' personnel prior to the introduction of the divisional scimitar and swastika patch. Note also the early use of maroon fezzes and Styrian gaiters.

ABOVE: The field-gray fez with dark-green tassel was issued by members of the Moslem SS divisions 'Handschar' and 'Kama' instead of the Einheitsfeldmütze. Traditionally, Moslem troops wore the peakless fez, and even brimless steel helmets during World War I, so that they could press their foreheads to the ground during prayer without removing their regulation headgear.

RIGHT: SS soldiers lie where they fell, killed during the horrendous fighting on the Eastern Front. It is likely that the Soviets staged this shot to show as many SS insignia as possible, thereby indicating that the Waffen-SS was not the invincible force which Nazi propaganda had portrayed.

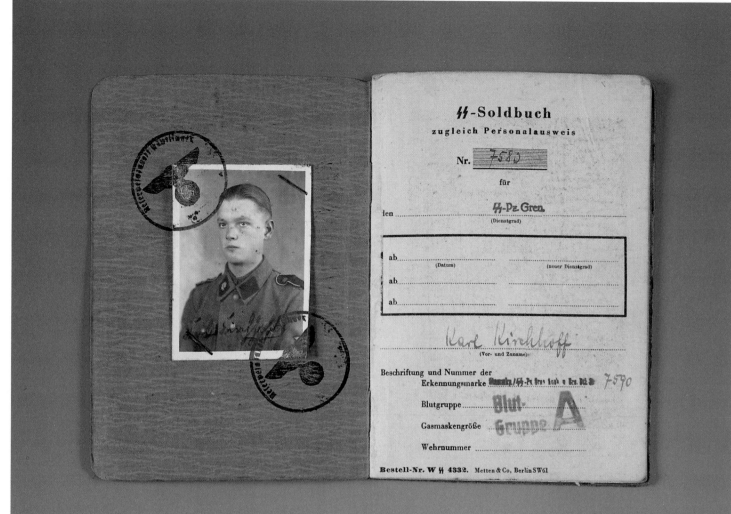

LEFT: The Waffen-SS Soldbuch, or paybook, doubled as an identity document and had to be carried by the holder at all times. Important details of service and current unit were listed within, and troops were given strict orders to remove and destroy the relevant pages before surrendering.

RIGHT: 'Handschar' artillery personnel during training, spring 1944.

BELOW: Three 'Handschar' troopers, wearing their distinctive scimitar and swastika collar patches. The name 'Handschar' was derived from an Arabic word meaning 'scimitar'.

BELOW RIGHT: SS-Brigadeführer Karl Sauberzweig, commander of the 'Handschar' Division, giving instructions to his driver in 1944. He wears the mountain-troop Edelweiss on his right sleeve. The Croat checkerboard shield of the division is also visible below the arm eagle of the officer standing at the driver's door.

formed well, but those from the east were poor at best, and at worst a complete rabble. Their loyalty was always in question and Himmler regarded them simply as racially inferior cannon-fodder, whose only other saving grace was their propaganda value.

As the war progressed, the vast majority of Waffen-SS uniform clothing was being manufactured 'in house' at concentration camps and prisons, many of which had fully equipped tailoring workshops or Be-

kleidungswerke. Their products bore the stamp 'SS-BW' followed by a code number allocated to the particular establishment concerned, an example being 'SS-BW-0-0453-0058' which related to Dachau. By 1944-45, however, shortages of raw materials had created such a crisis in the uniform industry that even the concentration camps could not meet the clothing needs of the Waffen-SS. The result was that newly recruited front-line SS soldiers ended up wearing captured uniforms,

particularly Italian items taken after the fall of Mussolini. Older veterans tended to retain their better-quality early-issue tunics, caps and boots for as long as possible, often until they quite literally fell apart. The uniforms and insignia of the Waffen-SS were distinct from those of the Allgemeine-SS, and can now be covered in some detail.

Headgear

The standard headgear of the armed SS formations continually evolved from 1933 until the end of World War II, with every year seeing either a new pattern being introduced, an existing style being modified, or an outdated item being withdrawn. In March 1933 members of the SS Stabswache Berlin, the forerunner of the Leibstandarte, were issued with heavyweight 1916- and 1918-model ex-army steel helmets, hand-painted or sprayed black, for wear when on guard duty. These plain Stahlhelme, which did not bear any SS insignia at that time, were the first distinguishing items of headgear to be sported by the armed units.

During the summer of 1933, field caps identical in cut to those of the Imperial German army were distributed for wear during training and fatigues. Known as 'Krätz-

chen' or 'scratchers' because of their rough texture, these black cloth caps were of the peakless 'pork pie' type, circular in cut with white piping. They bore a metal 1929-pattern eagle and swastika above a Prussian Totenkopf and featured a waterproof rust-brown fabric interior with a thin leather sweatband.

Early in 1934, the *Reichszeugmeisterei der NSDAP* or

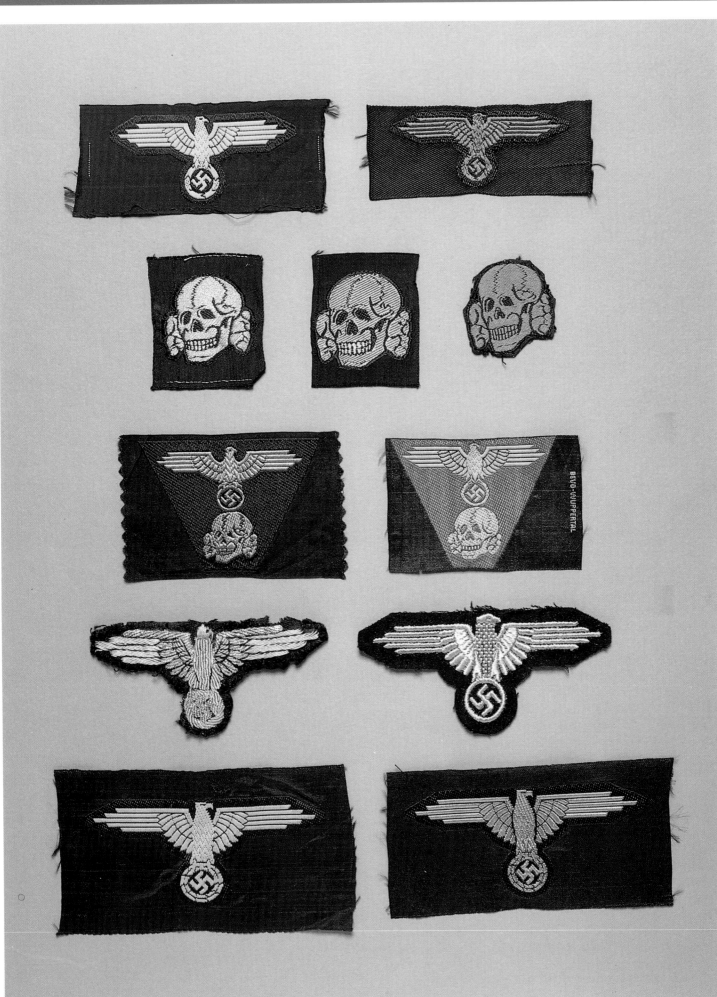

LEFT: The model-1935 steel helmet worn by police combat units, and by the SS-Polizei-Division until 1942.

BELOW: The model-1942 Waffen-SS steel helmet, clearly showing its distinctive sharp silhouette.

BOTTOM: This unique version of the M42 helmet, in black with white stenciled insignia, is believed to have been worn by Allgemeine-SS Alarmstürme units during the spring of 1945, when engaged in front-line defense fighting with the Volkssturm. It is the only known surviving example.

RIGHT: A Schutzpolitzei officer's shako, with white horsehair parade plume. This form of headgear was frequently worn on ceremonial occasions before the war.

RZM, the Nazi party's contracts office, placed an order for the supply of new SS helmets to replace the 1916/18 models which were considered unnecessarily heavy for the armed SS, whose main role was then one of internal security rather than open warfare. The RZM-pattern helmet was made of light chromium steel alloy, was marginally less angular in shape and had an improved liner. There were two inspection marks die-stamped into the neck of the helmet, SS runes on the left side, and the RZM symbol on the right. The RZM helmet was popular, but was suited only to parade and guard duty and was not widely distributed. On 23 February the same year, special insignia was introduced for wear on all SS steel helmets, hand-painted at first and then in decal form. The Leibstandarte was authorized to use white SS runes on a black shield (soon replaced by black SS runes on a silver shield) on the right side of the helmet, and an army-pattern shield bearing the national colors of black, white and red in diagonal bars on the left side. Troops of the PBs, and their successors in the SS-VT, wore white-bordered black runes within a white double circle on the right side of the Stahlhelm, and a white-bordered black swastika on the left side. That December, SS helmets began to be painted in so-called 'earth-gray', a gray-brown shade, for military maneuvers, and an other-ranks' field cap in an identical color was introduced to replace the 'Krätzchen'. The 1934-pattern cap was again intended for drill use only and was shaped like an upturned boat, hence its nickname 'Schiffchen' or 'little ship'. Its design was based on the army forage cap first issued about the same time, with a scalloped front and side panels which could be lowered to protect the wearer's ears in cold weather. The first 'Schiffchen' were issued with a machine-embroidered version of the 1929-pattern eagle on the left side and a plain white metal button to the front.

ABOVE: The black SS service cap, shown here in its three forms for NCOs/men, officers and generals, was seldom worn after 1939.

LEFT: The wartime Schirmmütze of an SS general, with aluminum piping and zinc-alloy insignia.

BELOW LEFT: An M42 steel helmet, clearly showing the SS runes decal.

RIGHT: Soldiers of the Polizei-Division in training, April 1940. Note the use of police steel helmets, and the mixture of police collar patches with Waffen-SS shoulder straps and arm eagles.

BELOW RIGHT: After 1940, most black SS service caps were stripped of their insignia and re-issued to the Germanic-SS in western Europe.

Soon after its introduction, however, the plain button was changed to one featuring an embossed 1934-pattern SS death's head.

In March 1935, troops of the SS-Wachverbände were authorized to wear a large silver-painted Prussian Totenkopf on the left side of the steel helmet, to distinguish them from the Leibstandarte and SS-VT. This insignia was short-lived though, for on 12 August 1935 a new set of standardized helmet badges was introduced for all SS units, to replace those previously worn. The new insignia, designed by Prof. Hans Haas, comprised black SS runes on a silver shield to be worn on the right side of the helmet, and a red shield bearing a white disk containing a black swastika to be worn on the left side. The original order decreed that these badges were to be painted on, but it was soon announced that they would be available in decal form. They were applied to all SS helmets in time for the NSDAP rally that September. Towards the end of the year, an earth-gray version of the black SS peaked cap was introduced for officers of the Leibstandarte and SS-VT, to be worn on all occasions when a steel helmet was not required. The new

LEFT: A Waffen-SS officer's classic 'old-style' or 'crusher' field cap, which was custom-made in Italy in 1943. It bears the trademark 'Successori Fare – Milano/Roma/ Toreno/Modena', and features a leather peak and narrower than usual black-velvet band.

BELOW LEFT: A black version of the 1934-pattern Schiffchen field cap, introduced in 1936 for use by armed SS enlisted men when walking out.

RIGHT: A model-1938 'crusher' field cap for NCOs, with regulation cloth peak. During the war, it was not uncommon for a mixture of insignia to be worn on headgear due to local shortages and supply difficulties. In this case, an old Prussian-style death's head has been used to replace a missing or damaged 1934-pattern Totenkopf.

Schirmmütze coincided with distribution of the new, lighter-model army steel helmet, with shallow neck guard, less protruding visor and simplified ventilation holes. Nevertheless, the old traditional 1916/18 models still continued to be worn for some considerable time, particularly by officers.

On 31 March 1936, the other-ranks' field cap began to be manufactured in a black version for wear with the black service uniform when walking out, and in earth-brown for SS-TV personnel on duty within concentration camps. Insignia remained the same, although the embroidered 1929-pattern eagle was replaced by the distinctive SS type later in the year. In 1937 there was a general distribution of a new field-gray combat uniform to all branches of the armed SS, with consequent changes in headgear. The earth-gray and earth-brown Schiffchen were replaced by a ubiquitous field-gray version, and the officer's peaked cap also began to be made with a field-gray top.

On 25 February 1938, a new field cap was created for NCOs. It was similar in appearance to the Schirmmütze, with a field-gray top, black cloth band and white piping, but the peak was made from the same cloth as the top of the cap and there was no chinstrap or stiffener. It could be folded for storage in the breadbag or rucksack, hence its nickname 'the crusher'. Many NCOs who later became officers continued to wear this popular cap throughout the war, and some individuals

hired private tailors to make variants of it with leather peaks, velvet bands and silk linings.

In 1939, a less elaborate version of the field-gray peaked cap was authorized for wear by NCOs in the vicinity of their barracks. It was only after the black uniform had ceased to be worn as walking-out dress that other ranks were issued with, or allowed to purchase, the field-gray peaked cap for walking out. That June, officers were permitted to buy a non-regulation white-topped Schirmmütze for wear with the new summer uniform.

The outbreak of war in September 1939 witnessed the first use by some rear-echelon SS units of the so-called *Edelstahlhelm*, which was manufactured from a thin-gauge steel and had previously been issued only to police and fire fighters. Soon afterwards, following army practice, an inverted chevron or soutache of braided piping in the appropriate branch of service color began to be worn on the front of the other ranks' field cap, above the death's head button which was thereafter painted field-gray. Armed SS officers still had no regulation field cap of their own, and during the first few months of the war many of them purchased the 1938-model army officer's forage cap and replaced or covered the national cockade with either a metal SS death's head or a small silver one removed from an army panzer collar patch. This obvious shortcoming in SS headgear was remedied in December 1939, however,

when a new field cap was authorized specifically for Waffen-SS officers. It was again boat-shaped, but did not have a scalloped front, and the side panels were gently sloping in the style of the Luftwaffe *Flieger-mütze*. The top of the flap was piped in aluminum cord and insignia consisted of the SS eagle and Totenkopf machine-woven in aluminum wire on a black ground. A Waffenfarbe soutache was worn over the death's head.

On 21 March 1940, the gaudy black, white and red swastika decal was ordered removed from SS steel helmets for the duration of the war, for camouflage reasons. That October, the other ranks' 1934-pattern field cap was replaced by a new style Schiffchen identical in cut to the officer's version. It became known as the *Feldmütze neuer Art* or 'new-model field cap', and featured a machine-woven eagle and death's head on the front of the cap instead of the death's head button and side eagle. December saw the issue of a *Bergmütze* or mountain cap to the fledgling Waffen-SS alpine units.

In February 1941, the manufacture and retailing of SS peaked caps was freed from RZM control. From then on, the Schirmmütze could be made to individual order by private hatters. A variety of makers' labels could subsequently be found inside SS peaked caps, and these were not restricted to German firms. A custom-made 'crusher' cap in the author's collection, for example, which was produced for a Leibstandarte officer stationed in Italy in 1943, bears the trademark 'Successori Fare – Milano/Roma/Toreno/Modena'. As a result of the ever-increasing difficulty in obtaining SS caps and insignia at the front line, many officers purchased army or police caps and replaced the badges with their own.

In March 1941, the 1916, 1918 and RZM model steel helmets, and any old stocks of earth-gray cloth headgear still in use, were ordered to be withdrawn from service. The following winter saw the first widespread use of fur caps, particularly captured Russian Ushankas, by the Waffen-SS. An almost indescribable range of official, semi-official and unofficial winter caps quickly developed, and the insignia utilized was entirely dependent upon what was available at the time. Metal Schirmmütze badges, cloth Feldmütze insignia, sleeve eagles and even death's heads cut from SS-Totenkopf-Division collar patches have been observed in photographs. On 1 August 1942, the smooth inward crimping of the steel helmet rim was abandoned for economic reasons, giving the model 1942 helmet a sharp silhouette. The next month, the soutache was dropped and no longer featured on the Schiffchen.

By 1943, practical experience at the front had shown the Schiffchen to be almost useless in comparison to the Bergmütze. On 1 October, therefore, a new field cap was introduced to replace all its predecessors. Known as the *Einheitsfeldmütze*, or standard field cap, it was very similar to the mountain cap, but had a longer peak and lower crown. Later versions featured only one fiber or plastic button at the front instead of two metal ones. Insignia was officially a woven death's head to the front and a woven eagle to the left side, but Schirmmütze badges were frequently used, and the eagle often appeared on the front. Later in the year, a one-piece triangular 'economy' insignia showing both the SS eagle and the Totenkopf was authorized, but it was not widely manufactured or distributed. On 1 November 1943 the SS runes helmet decal was discontinued for the duration of the war. The fez, or *Tarbusch*, was also introduced during 1943, for wear instead of the field cap by members of Moslem SS units. The fez was made from heavy field-gray felt, with a dark-green silken tassel and standard woven insignia. A version in maroon was sometimes sported by officers when walking out or on parade, but may have been unofficial. Albanian Moslems had their own conical fez.

In 1944, Italian SS formations made widespread use of former Italian Army field caps, peaked caps and steel helmets, with the addition of appropriate insignia, and in 1945 some Indian volunteers transferred from the Wehrmacht wore turbans with Waffen-SS uniform.

LEFT: Concentration-camp NCOs and guards in 1938. This picture illustrates a wide variety of uniform items, including the M34 Schiffchen, the M38 field cap, the black SS service cap, the drill uniform, and the earth-brown SS-Totenkopfverbände tunic.

ABOVE: Julius Schreck in 1933, wearing an early personalized version of the 'crusher' cap. The winged insignia below his ribbon bar is an Imperial Flying Club badge.

RIGHT: Maroon Tarbusch used by the first officers of the 'Handschar' division when walking out. Such items were converted from civilian fezzes, and were a temporary expedient pending issue of the official field-gray model.

Field Tunics

Members of the first armed SS units wore the 1932-pattern black service uniform on all occasions. It was identical to the outfit issued to the Allgemeine-SS, but while it was impressive when worn on parade or when walking out, it proved totally impractical for use in the field, or when performing general barrack duties. In order to protect the black uniform in such circumstances, tunics and trousers manufactured from a light-weight gray-white cotton drill were produced in the summer of 1933. Officers and NCOs subsequently wore a drill jacket which was cut very much like the black tunic, although sometimes with concealed buttons, and on which collar patches and a shoulder strap were worn. Other ranks had a less attractive, shapeless, badgeless tunic with a standing collar.

At the beginning of 1935 a new earth-gray uniform, identical in style to the black service outfit, began to be distributed to soldiers of the Leibstandarte and SS-VT. Enlisted men's tunics had five buttons down the front instead of four, and could be worn closed at the neck. Since the standard SS armband with its bright colors was clearly unsuitable for field use, it was replaced on the left arm of the earth-gray tunic by an eagle and swastika. In March 1936, an earth-brown version of the uniform was produced for everyday work wear by SS-Totenkopfverbände personnel on duty within the confines of concentration camps. In 1937, the earth-gray and earth-brown uniforms were replaced by a new standardized field-gray SS uniform. It was based on that of the army, but the jacket retained the typically SS features of slanting slash side pockets and a black/silver piped collar which was the same color as the rest of the tunic. The following year, the Leibstandarte began to be issued with army tunics, distinguished by their unpiped dark-green collars and pleated patch side pockets, for wear during training.

At the end of 1939, the sudden formation of the SS-Totenkopf-Division and the Polizei-Division necessi-

tated the widespread and general use of standard army-issue tunics since there were insufficient quantities of the SS-style field-gray uniform. Because of the basic differences in cut between the two patterns, and Himmler's desire for uniformity of dress, various contradictory orders were issued during the winter of 1939-40,

LEFT: Heinrich Schmauser, Führer of SS Oberabschnitt Süd, wearing the black service uniform in 1935.

BELOW, FAR LEFT: The Nazi movie-director Leni Riefenstahl with troopers of the Leibstandarte, sporting their new helmet decals, during the filming of the Reichsparteitag in 1935.

BELOW LEFT: In September 1940, Himmler visited the Leibstandarte at its barracks in Metz and presented Dietrich with a new Feldzeichen based on Hitler's personal standard.

RIGHT: The 1940-pattern tunic with field-gray collar, as worn by an artillery Rottenführer of the 'Götz von Berlichingen' Division, spring 1944. The ribbons are those of the Iron Cross 2nd Class and Russian Front Medal; the General Assault Badge and Wound Badge in Black are also displayed. The dress bayonet and knot were carried when walking out.

LEFT: A privately tailored army-pattern service tunic of a Waffen-SS infantry Untersturmführer, c. 1941.

ABOVE: Field uniform as worn by a Totenkopf Oberscharführer, c. 1943. The pleatless pockets were standard for this army M42 tunic, as was the reduction of the belt hook holes from three to two.

RIGHT: Field service dress of an infantry Obersturmführer, 3rd SS-Panzer Division 'Totenkopf', c. 1943. Of particular note are the piped Einheitsfeldmütze, and the obsolete 1938-pattern death's head cuff title denoting previous service with the 1st SS-Totenkopf-Standarte 'Oberbayern'. Map cases were issued to all officers, NCOs and dispatch riders.

instructing which outfits should be worn by officers as opposed to NCOs and other ranks, when they should be buttoned or unbuttoned at the neck, and so on. These orders were generally ignored by all concerned, and the result was a fair mixture of dress worn simultaneously within even the smallest units. In May 1940 army tunics began to make their inevitable appearance in the ranks of the SS-Verfügungsdivision, and they soon became universal throughout the Waffen-SS. During the course of 1940, their dark-green collars were phased out in favor of field-gray ones, and that August the black/silver collar piping was discontinued. From 1942, purely for reasons of economy, patch pockets were made without pleats and in 1943 the lower edges of the pocket flaps were straightened. The wool content of the model-1943 tunic was also drastically reduced, which

resulted in poor thermal insulation and a low tensile strength. On 25 September 1944 an entirely new style of field tunic based on the British Army battledress blouse was introduced for wear by all German ground combat units, including members of auxiliary formations such as the RAD and NSKK. A universal color called 'Feldgrau 44', which was more slate-gray than field-gray, was devised for the new outfit in an effort to standardize the various military and paramilitary uniform colors hitherto seen on the battlefield. However, in reality, many different shades of it emerged. The 1944 field uniform was very unpopular, and was not issued in sufficient quantities to change the appearance of the Waffen-SS radically.

The uniform regulations for Waffen-SS officers differed somewhat from those for other ranks. Until 1939

LEFT: During the war, members of the plain-clothes security police serving in the occupied territories were afforded the protection of wearing the gray uniform of the Sicherheitsdienst, irrespective of whether or not they were members of the SD or, indeed, of the SS. The blank right-hand collar patch and 'SD' sleeve diamond, originally denoting attachment to the old SD-Hauptamt, eventually became universal throughout the Sipo and SD. The regulation Allgemeine-SS 1938-pattern tunic also sports the War Merit Cross 1st and 2nd Classes, frequently awarded to the security police for their 'special services'.

RIGHT: Service tunic of a Schutzpolizei Oberleutnant, c. 1943. Himmler planned to merge the SS and police into a single Staatsschutzkorps, or State Protection Corps, and to that end encouraged dual membership of both organizations. Police officers accepted into the SS were distinguished by the wearing of Sig-Runes in bullion embroidery below the left breast pocket.

officers in the Leibstandarte and SS-VT had only one field-gray tunic, the 'Rock', which was identical in cut to the black SS service tunic and was always worn open at the neck with a brown shirt and black tie. At the beginning of the war, some SS officers avoided the expense of having to buy a field blouse for combat wear by having their existing tunics converted, with the addition of stand-and-fall collars which could be closed at the neck. Others had dark-green open-necked collars fitted, even though that was expressly forbidden. A number of similar stop-gap measures were taken until the issue of a general order in December 1939, which stipulated that officers' field tunics were henceforth to be identical in style to those of other ranks. Throughout the remainder of the war, Waffen-SS officers generally wore either privately-tailored field blouses like those of their army colleagues, or basic-issue tunics purchased from their unit stores. White summer versions were also produced,

although these were officially prohibited in June 1940, and the olive-green waterproof cotton duck from captured Soviet groundsheets was often made up into light-weight unlined field tunics for hot weather use.

While most Waffen-SS units were issued with one or more of these uniforms, depending upon the date of formation, the Italian SS alone, was not. At the end of 1943, SS-Obergruppenführer Karl Wolff, the Chief of the Hauptamt Persönlicher Stab RfSS and Supreme SS and Police Commander in Italy, successfully bargained with the army's Quartermaster-General for the supply of 100,000 captured Italian Army uniforms for wear by his SS and police anti-partisan forces. Many of these items were subsequently used to kit out the 24th and 29th Waffen-SS divisions, whose members duly sported a hodgepodge of Italian garb in gray-green, colonial khaki and Mediterranean camouflage, with their own unique Italian SS insignia.

Camouflage Clothing

The creation of standardized camouflage clothing was the most significant contribution of the Waffen-SS to the history of military-uniform development, and had a profound effect on the appearance of all modern soldiery. In February 1937 SS-Sturmbannführer Wilhelm Brandt, who was a Doctor of Engineering and commander of the SS-VT reconnaissance battalion, began work on the design of camouflage clothing and equipment for use by his troops. His prototype camouflage groundsheets (*Zeltbahnen*) and helmet covers were successfully tested by the SS-Standarte 'Deutschland' in field maneuvers the following December, during which it was estimated that they would reduce battle casualties by 15 percent. In June 1938, patents in respect of these items were granted to the Reichsführer-SS, so that they could not be copied by the army. By January 1939 despite great difficulties in obtaining sufficient quantities of waterproof cotton duck, and the fact that printing had to be hand-done, 8400 groundsheets and 6800 helmet covers had been supplied to the SS-Verfügungstruppe. Smocks were also distributed, and Hausser instructed that at least 20 of these should be held by each company for the exclusive use of assault troops.

Camouflage clothing was not widely worn during the Polish campaign, but even so the revolutionary SS Zeltbahnen and helmet covers earned high praise from Generalmajor Kempf, who sent samples of them to the Army High Command in Berlin for evaluation. By June 1940 hand-printing had been superseded by a much

LEFT: An early-pattern Waffen-SS camouflage smock, with vertical openings at the front, an absence of foliage loops, and no pockets in the skirt. It is shown summer-side out, with green predominating.

ABOVE: Waffen-SS recruiting poster, *c.* 1943. The artist, Mjölnir, apparently did not do his homework, since the Leibstandarte Feldzeichen is inaccurate, and the SS runes are worn on the wrong collar patch and on the wrong side of the steel helmet!

RIGHT: An SS officer, wearing the black panzer Einheitsfeldmütze, interrogating captured Allied paratroopers at Arnhem, September 1944.

LEFT: A late-pattern SS camouflage smock, distinguished by the foliage loops at the shoulders and pockets in the skirt. It is shown fall-side out, and is accompanied by a matching helmet cover.

RIGHT: A Soviet tank crew surrendering to an SS NCO wearing the camouflage smock and field cap, summer 1943.

FAR RIGHT: Assault troops of the SS-Verfügungsdivision, identifiable by their lack of collar patches, sporting newly issued camouflage smocks and helmet covers in May 1940.

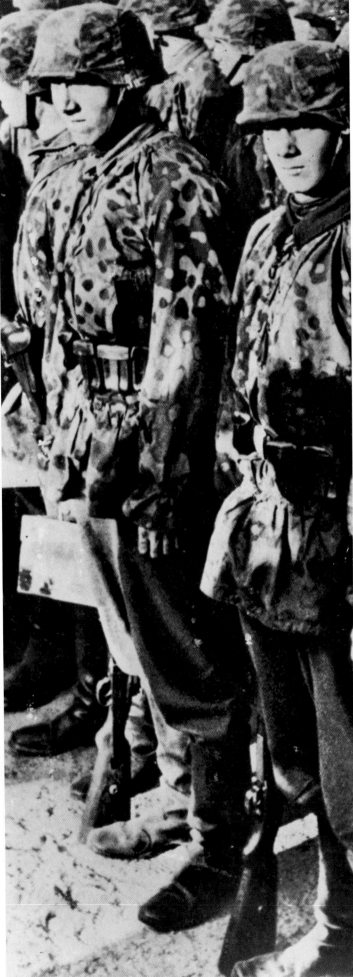

faster machine process which allowed mass production of 33,000 smocks for delivery to all field units of the Waffen-SS. Many variant styles of camouflage were ultimately manufactured simultaneously and issued indiscriminately throughout the Waffen-SS. Most garments made from waterproof cotton duck were printed on both sides and were reversible, with one side predominantly green and the other brown for use as seasonal variations dictated.

The Zeltbahn was the first item of camouflage uniform to see widespread distribution. It was triangular in shape, measuring 203cm × 203cm × 240cm, and could be worn as a cape or poncho, or buttoned together with three others to form a four-man tent. In fact, any number of groundsheets could be combined to make even larger shelters. When attaching Zeltbahnen in such circumstances, care had to be taken to use identical, or at least similar, pattern groundsheets to maintain the camouflage effect, and to that end identifying numbers were printed along their bases. Even when combining shelter quarters of different designs, 'paving slabs' of color were provided along the edges at regular intervals so that the various camouflage patterns would merge into each other. In December 1943 it was decided not to issue any more groundsheets to men on the eastern front for economy reasons, and by September 1944 their production had ceased completely.

LEFT: Summer uniform of a Leibstandarte Sturmbannführer, c. 1940. This order of dress was authorized in June 1939 for wear between 1 April and 30 September each year, but was seldom used other than during ceremonial occasions at Berchtesgaden. Note in particular the black piping to the peaked cap, and the German Horseman's Badge on the left breast pocket.

RIGHT: Police field-service uniform as worn by a Hauptmann of Gendarmerie, c. 1944. The rural police, distinguished by its orange piping and brown leatherwork, covered landward and mountainous districts of the Reich and also supervised prisoners-of-war engaged in agricultural work. It was commanded by SS-Gruppenführer August Meyszner. This outfit features an adjutant's aiguillette, an Old Campaigner's chevron, SS breast runes, the German National Sports Badge in Silver, the War Merit Cross and, interestingly, the basic NSDAP-membership badge pinned to the left breast pocket, a fairly common practice amongst the civil police during wartime. Note also the blue ribbon of a police long-service decoration, with miniature eagle.

LEFT: The definitive Waffen-SS M43 winter parka, made from two layers of windproof material. It was fully reversible, being white on one side and fall-camouflaged on the other, and the hood was large enough to be worn over the steel helmet.

RIGHT: The parka was issued with matching pants and mittens, the latter accommodating a 'trigger finger'.

The steel-helmet cover was produced from segments of Zeltbahn material, and consequently occasionally featured the identifying printed pattern number. It was designed to conform to the shape of the model-1935 Stahlhelm and was attached by means of three spring-loaded blackened steel clips held on by bare aluminum rivets, one at each side and one at the rear. Covers made from 1942 onwards had loops sewn on to hold foliage.

The camouflage smock was a reversible pullover garment gathered at the neck by means of an adjustable cord and at the wrists and waist by elastic. It had no collar and the first pattern had no pockets, only two vertical openings at the front which gave the wearer access to his tunic underneath. During the war, various modifications were made to it including the adoption of a longer 'skirt', foliage loops sewn in threes to the shoulders and upper sleeves, and the addition of two side pockets with buttoned flaps. However, all smocks conformed to the standard manufacturing process of being cut out from a long strip of Zeltbahn material, with a central hole for fitting over the head. They were sewn only up the sides, never across the shoulders. Production ceased in January 1944, although smocks continued to be worn widely until the end of the war.

On 15 April 1942 a camouflage face mask, which had initially been rejected by Hausser during prewar trials, was issued for use in conjunction with the helmet cover and smock. It comprised a series of strings fitted to an elasticated strap and hung like a curtain over the face. The mask was very effective when used in bushy terrain and was much prized by snipers. The following June, a camouflage field cap, again made from waterproof Zeltbahn material, was introduced. It was shaped like the Bergmütze and was generally unlined and reversible. From December 1942, special insignia woven in green and brown artificial silk were produced for wear on the cap, but were not widely adopted.

On 1 March 1944 a camouflage version of the drill uniform was introduced for both field and working dress. It comprised a tunic and trousers in the same cut as the model-1943 field uniform, but made from lightweight unlined herringbone twill with a standardized spotted or 'pea' pattern camouflage printed on one side only. It could be worn on its own during the summer, or on top of a standard field uniform in cold weather, and was designed to replace the more expensive smock and, ultimately, the normal field and drill uniforms. Only the eagle and swastika and special rank badges were intended to be worn on the left sleeve of the tunic, but shoulder straps and other insignia were also occasionally seen. Between 1 November 1944 and 15 March 1945, distribution of the camouflage drill uniform was suspended because of its intolerable losses during the winter months. In effect, it was never reissued.

LEFT: A pre-1942 camouflage helmet cover, distinguished by its lack of foliage loops. The spring-loaded blackened steel clips were held in place by bare aluminum rivets.

BELOW: Special rank insignia comprising bars and oakleaves, either embroidered or printed, were authorized for wear on camouflage uniforms without shoulder straps. Those shown relate to Obergruppen-führer, Oberführer and Hauptsturmführer.

RIGHT: Two Waffen-SS prisoners in Normandy, July 1944. The Obersturmführer on the left wears pants made from captured Italian camouflage material.

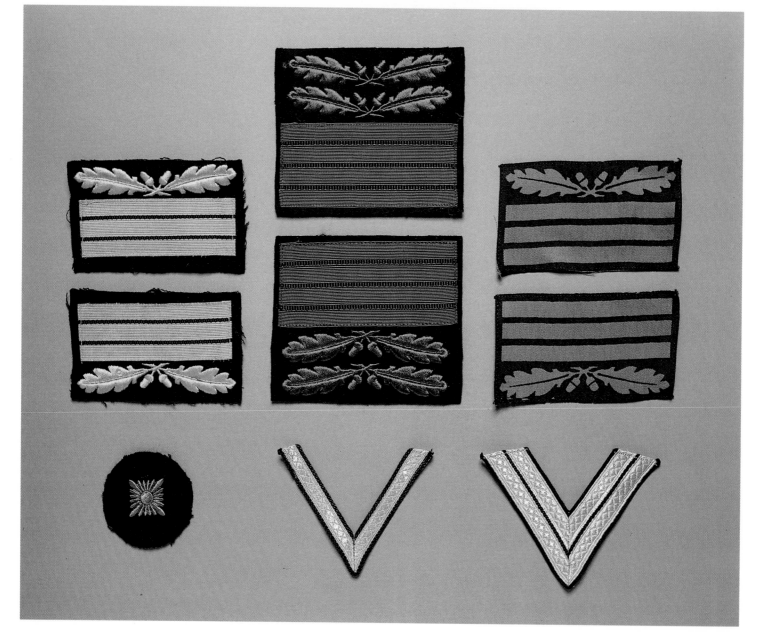

LEFT: An M44 'pea'-pattern camouflage drill tunic, as worn by a Waffen-SS NCO.

RIGHT: It was not uncommon for SS officers and men to display full rank insignia and decorations on the camouflage drill tunic, contrary to regulations. In this case, infantry Obersturmführer shoulder straps are clearly evident and a range of awards is worn, most notably the Knight's Cross of the Iron Cross at the neck, and the Close Combat Clasp above the ribbon bar. The officer's buckle is the pre-1942 nickel-silver type, as opposed to the later matt-gray alloy version which has been widely reproduced. Note also the 'WIF'-pattern field torch hanging from the right breast pocket, and the privately purchased binoculars by Carl Zeiss.

Panzer Uniforms

SS-VT armored troops received their version of the black panzer uniform in 1938. Its special headgear took the form of a floppy black woolen beret, or *Baskenmütze*, fitted over an internal crash helmet, the *Schutzmütze*, which comprised a heavily-padded liner. A large embroidered SS eagle and a uniquely designed Totenkopf, not unlike the army's panzer death's head but with a lower jaw in the SS style, were sewn to the front of the beret. The Baskenmütze was discontinued in 1940 after proving impractical in combat. It was replaced by a black version of the Schiffchen field cap, which in turn was superseded by a black Einheitsfeldmütze in October 1943. The SS tank tunic, or *Panzerjacke*, was a short, double-breasted black jacket fastened with concealed buttons. It differed from its army counterpart in that the front was cut vertically instead of being slanted, the lapels were smaller, and there was no central seam down the back. The collar of the jacket was piped in silver for officers but was unpiped for other ranks.

In the spring of 1941, a field-gray version of the panzer uniform was issued to members of the Leibstandarte's Sturmgeschütz-Abteilung. By August 1942 this outfit had been distributed to other assault-gun units, and four months later its wear was extended to all Waffen-SS anti-tank formations. A lightweight panzer uniform in reed-green denim drill material was issued to crews of tanks and armored cars to be worn as a work or summer outfit. It was instantly popular and remained so throughout the war. There were minor modifications made at various stages, such as the addition of large patch pockets with flaps to the left front of the jacket and left thigh of the trousers.

On 15 January 1943, panzer crews received a one-piece combination work uniform made of camouflage waterproof cotton duck, identical to the material used in the manufacture of the smock and Zeltbahn. These coveralls were usually worn without insignia, although shoulder straps were occasionally sported. At the same time a winter combination made from two thicknesses of cloth, white on one side and field-gray on the other, was introduced and was widely worn during the battle

FAR LEFT: An SS panzer outfit for a Leibstandarte Hauptsturmführer, *c.* 1943.

LEFT: An M36 army-pattern tunic with dark-green collar, as worn by a Rottenführer of the SS-Totenkopf-Division, *c.* 1941. The standard-issue Kar.98k rifle ammunition pouches, or Patronentaschen, dated from 1915 and remained virtually unchanged until 1945. Each set comprised three compartments holding a total of 30 rounds in six clips.

ABOVE: An M43 Waffen-SS panzer Einheitsfeldmütze, with the one-piece woven insignia which was not issued until the last months of the war.

RIGHT: The rounded lapels and vertically-cut front of the SS Panzerjacke are clearly evident from this tank tunic of a 'Das Reich' Unterscharführer, *c.* 1944. Of particular note are the pink Waffenfarbe piping to the shoulder straps, the Tank Battle Badge in Silver, and the method of wearing the ribbon of the Iron Cross 2nd Class from the left lapel.

LEFT: Obersturmbannführer Kurt Meyer as commander of the Leibstandarte reconnaissance battalion in Russia, July 1941. He is wearing a 'crusher' cap with an early Prussian death's head. Meyer was one of the 'boy generals' of the Waffen-SS, ultimately winning the Knight's Cross with Oakleaves and Swords while leading the 'Hitlerjugend' Division in Normandy. His daring exploits earned him the nickname 'der Schnelle Meyer' ('quick Meyer'), and later 'Panzermeyer' ('tank Meyer').

RIGHT: Troops of the 2nd SS-Panzergrenadier Regiment taking Stoumont in the Ardennes, 19 December 1944.

of Kharkov. These coverall combinations were never very popular, simply because of the difficulty of getting in and out of them. That fact, allied with the success of the reed-green denims and the extreme shortage of waterproof cotton duck, led to the decision being made in January 1944 to discontinue the camouflage combination and produce instead a lightweight version of the panzer uniform in camouflage herringbone twill. It duly appeared two months later, at the same time as the camouflage drill uniform introduced for all other Waffen-SS units, and it was in the same standardized spotted 'pea' pattern, unlined and printed on one side only. The camouflage panzer uniform saw widespread service, particularly on the western front. On 1 November distribution ceased for the duration of the winter, and the camouflage outfit was never reissued.

While the clothing of Waffen-SS armored personnel remained fairly standard, there was one major initiative at divisional level which drastically altered the appearance of many panzer crews participating in the Normandy Campaign. During the autumn of 1943, the Leibstandarte had been involved in disarming capitulated Italian armed forces and fighting partisans in northern Italy. In the process, the division had confiscated huge quantities of abandoned Italian uniforms, among which were large numbers of German U-Boat leather jackets and trousers, originally sold by Hitler to Mussolini's navy, and vast stocks of Italian Army camouflage material. The latter was quickly used to produce caps, tunics and coveralls in the German style, which were distributed to soldiers of the Leibstandarte

and 'Hitlerjugend' in France. The U-Boat clothing went almost exclusively to the young tank crews of 'Hitlerjugend', and protected many of them against serious burns.

Paratroop Uniforms

SS-Fallschirmjäger-Bataillon 500 was formed at the end of 1943, in the wake of Otto Skorzeny's much-vaunted liberation of the deposed Mussolini that September, which had relied heavily on Luftwaffe paratroop support. Contrary to widespread belief, the SS paratroop battalion was not a penal unit but was composed entirely of volunteers. Its first major action took place in May 1944, and involved the battalion being dropped by glider right on top of Marshal Tito's vast partisan-headquarters complex in the mountains near Drvar, Yugoslavia. In the fighting which ensued, the unit was almost wiped out. The survivors were reformed as SS-Fallschirmjäger-Bataillon 600, under Skorzeny's command, and trained for a drop on Budapest to capture the son of the recalcitrant Hungarian leader, Admiral Horthy. Some SS paratroopers were later involved in the Ardennes Offensive, and the remainder fought as infantry on the eastern front. It is safe to say that the SS paras were always thrown into the worst hot-spots, and the battalion was thought of as something of a 'suicide squad'.

Of all the branches of the Waffen-SS, least is known about the clothing and equipment of the parachutists. It appears that the Luftwaffe assumed responsibility not only for the training and transportation by air of the SS paras, but also for supplying them with specialist dress and equipment. When Skorzeny and his small joint SS and Luftwaffe commando force rescued Mussolini from his imprisonment at Gran Sasso, they all wore regulation air-force tropical clothing with full Luftwaffe insignia. At a celebratory rally held in the Berlin Sports Palace soon afterwards, however, the SS men reverted to their normal field-gray uniforms.

The members of SS-Fallschirmjäger-Bataillone 500 and 600 wore 1940-pattern SS Schiffchen field caps, SS belt buckles and standard Waffen-SS field-gray tunics with the insignia of their previous units, since there were no specialist SS paratroop badges. The Luftwaffe supplied all their protective clothing, which comprised: the normal paratroop steel helmet, with or without Luftwaffe decal and 'splinter'-pattern cover; the 'splinter'-pattern camouflage paratroop jump smock, with or without Luftwaffe breast eagle; blue-gray or field-gray paratroop trousers; canvas gaiters; and ankle boots. One surviving photograph shows two German paratroopers wearing standard SS-issue camouflage smocks, but these are thought to be Luftwaffe Fallschirmjäger personnel in Italy, who would have had the opportunity of obtaining SS smocks from the 'Hermann Göring' panzer division, which was kitted out with them. Another unique picture illustrates an SS paratrooper apparently wearing the 'pea'-pattern camouflage drill tunic and trousers while fulfilling an infantry role on the eastern front near the end of the war.

During recent years, several references have been made to a batch of paratroop jump smocks manufactured from SS 'pea'-pattern camouflage drill material with the SS eagle stitched to the right breast. These appeared in the USA during the early 1980s with the story that they had been found by American troops

ABOVE: Sturmbannführer Otto Skorzeny, commander of the SS Special Forces, who was, for obvious reasons, dubbed 'scarface' by the American wartime press.

LEFT: On 12 September 1943, Skorzeny's SS commandos, with air-force support, carried out a daring glider-borne assault on the Hotel Campo Imperatore atop the Gran Sasso, the loftiest peak in the Apennines, and rescued Mussolini, who had been imprisoned there following his recent overthrow. All of those taking part wore Luftwaffe uniforms, with no indication of SS membership.

occupying the SS clothing depot at Dachau in April 1945. While such tales cannot be disproved, there must be grave doubts as to the authenticity of these items. For one thing, many are date-stamped '1943', a year early for 'pea'-pattern camouflage. Some stocks of 'pea'-pattern material survived the war, and it is now being reprinted for the battle re-enactment fraternity, so the postwar creation of 'SS para smocks' would not have been difficult, a point reinforced by the sudden appearance of a pair of never-before-heard-of SS paratroop camouflage trousers in France in 1990. No wartime references to, or photographs of, the SS paratroop smock exist. The so-called 'SS-Fallschirmjäger' cuff title is most certainly a postwar fantasy piece. No SS para cuff title was approved during the Third Reich, and the few titles worn by some SS paratroops were those of their former units.

Tropical Clothing

While Waffen-SS troops never served in North Africa, a few units, primarily the Leibstandarte, 'Wiking', 'Prinz Eugen' and 'Reichsführer-SS' saw action in the Balkans, southern Russia and Italy, where sweltering summer conditions made the wearing of conventional uniform items very uncomfortable. However, the demand for hot-weather clothing was usually localized and temporary, so the development of a tropical uniform for the Waffen-SS was gradual and on something of an *ad hoc* basis.

The first requirement for tropical clothing was voiced in April 1941, during the hastily organized invasion of Greece. Some members of the Leibstandarte took to wearing the basic SS sports kit, comprising undershirt and shorts, when not engaged in combat, while others went bare-chested. A short-term partial solution was achieved by the issue of army pith helmets, or *Tropenhelme*, but these were unpopular and were not worn in any great numbers. When sported by the SS, they bore no insignia. A number of original pith helmets survive featuring metal SS runic and swastika shield badges in the same style as the standard SS steel helmet decals. However, it is likely that these insignia are postwar creations, particularly since the swastika shield decal had been discontinued in March 1940, a year before the introduction of Tropenhelme to the SS. During the autumn of 1942, SS-Division 'Wiking' advanced deep into the Caucasus region, and a number of its personnel wore Luftwaffe tropical uniforms and Schiffchen field caps in light-tan cotton drill. Air-force insignia were replaced by SS badges, and from February 1943 SS rank chevrons in tan-brown on black were authorized for wear with the tropical tunic by Sturmmann/Rottenführer grades. At the same time, the use of collar patches with tropical gear was forbidden.

In September 1943, a wholly new and, for the first time, formalized Waffen-SS tropical uniform was introduced and distributed on an entire unit basis to the Sturmbrigade 'Reichsführer-SS' on Corsica. The uniform was a strange hybrid and may, in fact, have been made by converting Italian clothing which had recently been seized by the Germans. The tunic had pleated patch pockets in the army style, was colored light tan in the Luftwaffe style, and featured a caped effect across the upper section in the Italian Sahariana style, the peaks of the 'cape' forming the upper pocket flaps. Insignia was officially restricted to shoulder straps, tropical sleeve chevrons and a special tan-brown woven version of the SS arm eagle, but normal collar patches were also occasionally seen. The SS tropical field cap, to accompany the new tunic, was in the same shape as the SS camouflage field cap, without flap and buttons. It too was light tan in color and sported a tan-brown eagle and death's head. No officer's version existed.

Photographic evidence suggests that the 1943-pattern Waffen-SS tropical tunic was only ever issued to the Sturmbrigade 'Reichsführer-SS', and even then was not worn by members of that formation after they left Corsica. The Sturmbrigade appears to have been chosen to field-test and evaluate the new tunic on an experimental basis. Whether it was badly reported upon, or whether economies and the lack of tropical campaigns after 1943 dictated that no more stocks of the tunic would be manufactured, is unknown. In any event, there is nothing to indicate that it was issued again. The SS tropical field cap, on the other hand, was widely distributed among the various units fighting in Italy during 1944-45, and was a popular item of dress.

During the last year of the war, members of SS units in Italy, Austria and the Balkans reverted to wearing a mixture of Wehrmacht and Italian tropical clothing. Luftwaffe items were most prized, particularly the tunic and Schiffchen, and the latter could often be seen bearing SS metal badges removed from the peaked cap.

Protective Clothing

As early as July 1935, the Leibstandarte was issued with an earth-gray double-breasted greatcoat, or *Mantel*, which bore collar piping and full insignia. This item was superseded by a field-gray version in 1937, and with the military development of the SS-VT and SS-TV there was a tendency to follow army greatcoat fashions closely, which led to the gradual adoption of a dark-green collar and the *ad hoc* removal of collar patches. By the outbreak of war, the situation as regards greatcoat insignia was fairly muddled and various orders were issued in an attempt to clarify the position. The dark-green collar was officially approved in December 1939, only to be canceled a few months later. Collar piping for other ranks became obsolete in August 1940, and all surviving examples of the old earth-gray coat were recalled in March 1941. Officers with the rank of SS-Oberführer and above were permitted to wear the greatcoat with the top three buttons undone, so as to expose their distinctive silver-gray lapels, and from 1941 holders of the Knight's Cross and other neck awards were also allowed to do so. As the war progressed, many officers countered the declining quality of the issue Mantel by having greatcoats tailor-made to their own specifications. These items incorporated such refinements as removable blanket linings, reinforced buttons, extra pockets and detachable sheepskin or fur collars. The result of all this was that dozens of variations

LEFT: A defensive position on the Eastern Front during the winter of 1941-42. The soldiers wore basic army-pattern greatcoats, which afforded little protection in temperatures falling below −50°C.

BELOW: Hitler reviewing the Leibstandarte at its parade ground at Berlin-Lichterfelde, December 1935. The soldiers are kitted out with the new earth-gray Mantel, while the Führer sports a civilian leather greatcoat.

RIGHT: A black greatcoat with white belt and cross-strap, as worn on cold-weather ceremonial occasions by the Leibstandarte, c. 1937-39.

on the basic Waffen-SS greatcoat came to be produced
and worn side-by-side, many of them in direct contravention of regulations. Moreover, a massive version of
the Mantel, called the surcoat or *Übermantel*, was designed to be worn on top of the ordinary greatcoat by
drivers of open motor vehicles or those on static sentry
duty, and featured two vertical pockets above the waist,
in addition to the normal side pockets.

Officers had the option of purchasing a field-gray
leather greatcoat, but this item was extremely expensive and few subalterns could afford it. There were
several variants, both in cut and in the use of insignia.
As an alternative to the leather coat, many junior
officers and NCOs bought the much cheaper 1938-
pattern field-gray raincoat, the so-called *Regenmantel*,
made of rubberized cotton twill with a leather-like
appearance. Others used the regulation motorcyclist's
coat, or *Kradschutzmantel*, which was first introduced
for army dispatch riders and eventually came to be
widely worn by a variety of Wehrmacht, Waffen-SS and
police personnel during inclement weather. Early
examples had a dark-green cloth collar, but after 1940
the whole coat was made from rubberized fabric. The
skirt could be divided and buttoned around the legs for
ease of use on the motorcycle.

Following the disastrous winter campaign of 1941-42,
when no adequate warm clothing was provided for Ger-

man soldiers fighting on the Russian front, preparations were made to design and supply appropriate uniform items with a view to averting a similar crisis. Various fur, sheepskin and lambswool waistcoats and caps were issued in the short term, and snow anoraks originally intended for mountain troops serving in Norway were diverted and shipped east. Wherever shortages were still apparent, captured Soviet winter clothing was used, augmented by civilian items collected in Germany.

Throughout 1942, the Waffen-SS developed its own winter combat uniform, or *Winter-Sonderbekleidung*, independent of the army. It consisted of a heavy, fur-lined parka-type coat in a waterproof cement-gray gabardine, with matching overtrousers. When snow lay on the ground, an undyed white cotton hooded smock and trousers were issued. These were designed to be worn on top of the parka and overtrousers and were readily washable. At the end of the year, a padded reversible parka in a waterproof rayon, white on one side and tan or reed-green on the other, was distributed for use as a windcheater.

The definitive Waffen-SS winter uniform did not enter service until 1943-44, and comprised a hood, jacket, trousers and mittens, all made from two layers of windproof material with a wool-rayon interlining.

The whole outfit was reversible, being white on one side and SS autumn camouflage on the other, and was designed to be worn over the normal field uniform. The white side tended to get filthy very quickly, which defeated its purpose, so troops were ordered to wear the uniform with the camouflage side out unless they were actually fighting in snow-covered terrain. During 1944, a small number of similar garments were made utilizing stocks of captured Italian camouflage material. Some of these were reversible and others were lined in fur or sheepskin.

The production of fur-lined items for the Waffen-SS was generally undertaken by the SS Eastern Industries Ltd., or Ostindustrie GmbH, which used local Jewish labor to manufacture uniforms and equipment from property and raw materials seized by the Germans. Winter clothing was a specialty of the SS-Bekleidungswerke in the Lublin area of Poland, primarily at the Poniatowa and Trawniki work camps. Fur garments removed from concentration-camp inmates throughout the Reich were ordered to be collected and forwarded to Lublin for reprocessing. It is a sad fact that many Waffen-SS soldiers unknowingly wore winter uniforms lined with fox-furs and stoles taken from old women who had died at Auschwitz, Majdanek, Sobibor and Treblinka.

ABOVE LEFT: Senior SS and 'Hitlerjugend' officers, fronted by Sepp Dietrich and Fritz Witt, observe the training of the 12th SS 'Hitlerjugend' Panzer Division, 1943. Note the variety of greatcoats and protective clothing in evidence.

LEFT: Russian troops on the Russian Front, March 1942. Their camouflage clothing covered many more layers of regulation and non-regulation cold-weather gear. At this time, effective winter clothing was something of a luxury in the Waffen-SS. Only later, as the war on the Eastern Front dragged on, would the SS receive adequate cold-weather combat kit.

RIGHT: A Royal Tiger Tank of the 1st SS Panzer Division in the Ardennes, December 1944. The officer standing at left wears the second-pattern camouflage smock and pants, as do many of his colleagues on the tank, but note the greatcoat partially visible underneath the gun barrel.

Insignia Production

While the majority of wartime Waffen-SS uniforms were made by SS factories, the insignia attached to them always tended to be manufactured by long-established private companies. That arrangement necessitated strict standardization and quality control, the administration of which was entrusted to the Reichszeugmeisterei or RZM, a body which had been set up as early as 1 April 1929 to supervise the production and pricing of all Nazi party uniform items. The basic functions of the RZM were to see that NSDAP contracts went to Aryan firms and to ensure that final products were of a high standard yet priced to suit the pocket of the average party member. It also acted as a 'clearing house' between manufacturers on the one hand, and wholesalers and retailers on the other. On 16 March 1935, contract numbers were introduced and awarded to every RZM-approved company, and after that date RZM numbers replaced makers' marks on all NSDAP accouterments. So the buttons, belt hooks, etc. of the Allgemeine-SS, which always remained an organ of the Nazi party, consistently featured RZM marks. Those of the Waffen-SS, however, which was in effect a State arm during the war, very seldom did. Waffen-SS insignia fell into several distinct categories, according to manufacture. Each of these will now be described in turn.

Metal badges such as eagles and death's heads for the peaked cap, Totenkopf buttons for the 1934-pattern field cap, shoulder-strap ciphers and rank pips were made in a variety of materials, dependent primarily upon date of production. The most common combinations were as follows:

1933-36: plated brass or plated tombakbronze;
1936-45: copper-plated aluminum with a surface wash or bare aluminum;
1939-45: painted or plated steel;
1942-45: plated or painted zinc;
1944-45: bare zinc.

In general terms the quality of metals used declined as the war progressed, but despite that, a good standard of overall finish and appearance was always maintained. Early to mid-war examples were usually crisply die-struck, with hollow backs bearing two or three flat prongs or round pins for attachment purposes. The reverse of these items tended to feature a mirror image of the obverse design. Late-war badges were often cast, with smooth concave backs.

Cap eagles and death's heads, which were common to both the Allgemeine-SS and Waffen-SS, normally bore RZM marks, either individually stamped onto the badge reverse or embossed into it as part of the die-striking or casting process. Typical examples were 'RZM M1/52' (Deschler & Sohn of Munich) and 'RZM M1/167' (Augustin Hicke of Tyssa bei Bodenbach). During the war, the format of RZM codes used on metal SS insignia changed, deleting the 'M1' prefix and adding a year suffix, e.g. 'RZM 499/41'. No list of these later codes is known to have survived, and so they have never been deciphered.

The earliest SS cloth badges were hand-embroidered,

LEFT: Woven or paper RZM labels were attached to most SS cloth insignia, at least until the early part of the war, in lieu of makers' trademarks. The labels on the rear of this armband denote that it has been made in accordance with the approved SS pattern by the firm holding contract number 21 of 1935.

RIGHT: Karl Wilhelm Krause, the Führer's personal SS orderly between 1934 and 1939, holds a small model of part of the planned new Reichs Chancellery for examination by Speer, Hitler, Schaub and the sculptor Josef Thorak, Munich railway station, 1937.

and this form of insignia was worn by soldiers of the armed SS during the 1933-35 period. Hand-embroidery could be in white or silver-gray cotton thread, fine aluminum wire or heavy silver bullion, with the latter two styles normally being reserved for officers. However, in September 1934 non-commissioned and enlisted ranks of the Leibstandarte and SS-VT were also authorized to wear aluminum wire insignia with the black uniform, to set them apart from their colleagues in the Allgemeine-SS. No two hand-embroidered badges were ever identical, since they were individually made. The embroidery was usually done over cardboard templates, which comprised thin cutouts of the relevant designs and which could vary slightly from one maker to another. Once the actual embroidery was completed, a paper or cloth backing was glued onto the reverse of each piece to prevent fraying. Badge companies generally employed women to do this work, or farmed it out to local seamstresses on a cottage-industry basis.

In 1936, when the RZM had become effectively organized under Reichszeugmeister Richard Büchner, machine-embroidered insignia began to be produced and widely distributed for wear by SS enlisted men and NCOs. This form of embroidery was cheap and quick to execute, and generally utilized white or silver-gray cotton thread on a black-woven badgecloth base. The thickness of the embroidery depended upon how the individual manufacturer's machine was adjusted, but it usually had a tightly-formed and raised appearance. The only exception was the flat chain-stitch embroidery which was sometimes employed on shoulder-strap badges. The producers of machine-embroidered insignia were normally fairly substantial firms, as only they could afford the expensive equipment involved in the manufacturing process. Such companies were rigidly controlled by the RZM, and their products had to carry labels bearing the relevant contract numbers. In addition to the standard RZM paper tags used by all NSDAP formations, a system of small black-and-white woven labels was devised specifically for SS items. Each bore the RZM symbol and SS runes together with the maker's contract number and year date, an example being 'RZM 21/36 SS'. Where a firm was engaged only in embroidery work, the letters 'St', denoting 'Stickerei' or 'embroiderer', were incorporated into the label, for example 'RZM St 459/36 SS'. It was not uncommon for two such labels to be attached to a single badge, particularly a cuff title, if two separate firms were involved in its manufacture due to subcontracting. One label would refer to the maker of the backing and the other to the embroiderer, and because of this, machine-embroidered insignia has come to be known as the 'RZM-style' by collectors.

Machine-woven badges were produced from 1939, using artificial silk and either cotton or fine aluminum wire. They had a very flat appearance and the manufacturing process, which could produce hundreds of identical insignia run off on a single continuous strip of ribbon-like material, allowed for the incorporation of very fine detail into the design. The principal producer of these badges was the Wuppertal-Barmen firm of Bandfabrik Ewald Vorsteher, whose trademark 'BEVO' has come to be used when referring to all machine-woven insignia.

The use of silk-screen printing in the manufacture of certain Waffen-SS badges was introduced in 1944 but was primarily restricted to foreign volunteer shields, war-auxiliary armbands and the special rank insignia

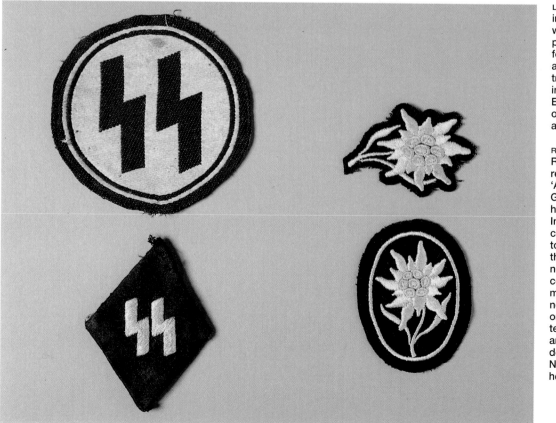

LEFT: Circular SS sports undershirt insignia, above the diamond badge worn on the upper left sleeve of the padded jacket by members of SS fencing teams. The Edelweiss was authorized for Waffen-SS mountain troops in October 1943, after the introduction of the ubiquitous Einheitsfeldmütze, and was used on the left side of the mountain cap and the right sleeve of the tunic.

RIGHT: On 13 August 1933, Himmler, Röhm and Seidel-Dittmarsch reviewed the first muster, or 'Appell', of SS Gruppe Ost at the German Stadium in Berlin. Himmler had joined the 11th Bavarian Infantry Regiment as an officer-cadet in January 1918, but was sent to the front just at the moment that the Armistice was concluded, and never saw action. He was painfully conscious of the fact that, unlike most of his contemporaries, he was not entitled to wear the Iron Cross or any other military award, and he tended to compensate for this by an overt display of NSDAP decorations, such as the 1929 Nürnberg Party Day Badge shown here on his left breast pocket.

for camouflage clothing. Cheap production costs were more than outweighed by the poor quality of the finished article, and printed badges were very unpopular.

The procedures governing the approval and manufacture of Waffen-SS insignia were very complicated. Various SS departments, particularly the SS Hauptamt, the SS Führungshauptamt, the SS Wirtschafts- und Verwaltungshauptamt and the Hauptamt Persönlicher Stab RfSS would often be involved. Once a design had been approved by Himmler, it would pass to the SS-WVHA which would in turn authorize the RZM to supply the required quantity. The RZM then placed a contract with one of its approved firms and the finished badges were delivered to one of the SS clothing depots, usually Dachau, from where they would be supplied to the unit concerned.

By September 1944, pressures on the RZM had developed to such an extent that it was forced to terminate its involvement in the supply of insignia to the Waffen-SS. The following December it announced that Waffen-SS eagles, death's heads, collar patches, shoulder straps and cuff titles could henceforth be manufactured, without a contract, for direct sale to authorized wholesalers and retailers for the duration of the war. By that stage, no less than 24 firms were producing cloth insignia for the Waffen-SS. These companies are listed below:

Gebrüder Auerhammer, Weissenburg; Albrecht Bender, Weissenburg; Max Dörfel, Eibenstock; Lothar von Dreden & Co., Wuppertal-Elberfeld; Oskar Frank, Eibenstock; Geissler & Hast, Ansbach; August Göbels Söhne, Gross-Schönau; E. Günther, Eibenstock; Hensel & Schuhmann, Berlin; Hinterleitner, Brunnacker & Co., Weissenburg; E. Köhler, Annaberg; Kruse & Söhne, Wuppertal-Barmen; Sigmund Lendvay, Vienna; Lucas & Vorsteher, Wuppertal-Barmen; F. Müller, Rossbach; R. Nitzsche, Eibenstock; J. F. Rieleder, Heilbronn; Julius Riess, Erfurt; Franz Rönnefahrt, Brandenburg; Hermann Schmuck & Co., Weissenburg; Thiele & Steinert, Freiberg; Tröltsch & Hanselmann, Berlin; Ewald Vorsteher, Wuppertal-Barmen; Ferdinand Winter, Treuchtlingen.

Waffenfarbe

During the Third Reich, certain colors were employed in the design of military, paramilitary and civil uniforms and accouterments as a methodical means of unit identification. These colors appeared on tunic facings, cap piping, armbands and so on and were known as branch of service colors or 'Waffengattungsfarben', normally referred to in the abbreviated form Waffenfarbe.

Before the outbreak of World War II, all armed SS piping was white, silver or black/silver twist, like that of the Allgemeine-SS. However, in December 1939, due to the increasing militarization of the Waffen-SS and its new-found associations with Wehrmacht forces, shoulder straps piped in army Waffenfarbe were in-

troduced. A few officers also began to equip themselves with Waffenfarbe-piped peaked caps and long trousers, made to order, but Himmler immediately forbade that practice, instructing that the piping on these items was to remain white. Some confusion then ensued, for in May 1940 the Reichsführer backtracked by indicating that peaked caps could thereafter be piped in Waffenfarbe, although all walking-out dress trousers were now to be piped in gray. The following November Himmler changed his mind yet again, directing that Waffenfarbe was once more to be restricted to shoulder straps and the soutache on the field cap, with all other piping reverting to white or aluminum depending on rank. It is clear that the Reichsführer wanted his soldiers to retain their own unique appearance, distinct from that of the army, but a number of Waffen-SS officers and men continued to wear Waffenfarbe on their peaked caps until the end of the war, in defiance of Himmler's orders.

The following list shows the Waffenfarbe colors

SS Waffenfarbe 1939-45

Waffenfarbe	Waffen-SS Branch of Service
Black	Construction Units
	Engineers
Dark (or 'Cornflower') Blue	Medical
Light Blue	Field Post Office (from Feb. 1943)
	Motor Technical School (until July 1942)
	Supply
	Transport (until August 1944)
Sky Blue	Administration
Copper Brown	Reconnaissance (until June 1942)
Light Brown	Concentration Camps
Dark Green	Reserve Officers (discontinued 1942)
	Specialists (until June 1942)
Grass Green	Mountain Troops (from May 1942)
	Police-Division (discontinued 1942)
Light Gray	General Officers
	Himmler's Staff (until June 1942)
Dark Gray	Himmler's Staff (from June 1942)
Orange	Field Police
	Garrison Troops
	Motor Technical School (from July 1942 until August 1944)
	Recruiting
	Technical Units
	Welfare
Light Pink	Motor Technical School (from August 1944)
	Transport (from August 1944)
Rose Pink	Panzer
	Anti-tank Troops
Salmon Pink	Military Geologists
Bright Red	Artillery
	Flak
	Rocket Units
Claret (or 'Bordeaux') Red	Legal Service
Crimson Red	Veterinary
Red/Gray Twist	Specialists (from June 1942)
White	Infantry
Golden Yellow	Cavalry
	Reconnaissance (from June 1942)
Lemon Yellow	Field Post Office (until Feb. 1943)
	Signals
	War Correspondents

RIGHT: Members of the 6th SS-Gebirgs Division 'Nord' captured on the Rhine front, March 1945. The Edelweiss is clearly shown on the right sleeve of the Unterscharführer in the center, who for some reason sports other-rank's shoulder straps. He also wears two-part cap insignia, even at this late stage in the war. Note too the use of shoulder straps with the camouflage drill tunic on the right, and the identity disk around the neck of the man on the left.

which were officially authorized for use by the Waffen-SS at various stages of World War II. However, it should be noted that a few shades were withdrawn or reallocated from time to time, and in any case the differences in some colors were so slight as to be almost indistinguishable, a situation compounded by variations in manufacturers' dyes, the bleaching effect of the sun and the general weathering of piping under field conditions. There is often heated debate between buyers and sellers of surviving piped items as to whether the Waffenfarbe colors concerned are rare or relatively common ones.

Collar Patches

The earliest armed SS units were technically on the local Abschnitte staff, and as such members wore blank right collar patches. In May 1933, officers' patches began to be piped in a black/aluminum twisted cord, and those of other ranks in white cord. With the rapid expansion of the militarized SS formations, it soon became clear that some kind of distinctive collar insignia was required for the Leibstandarte and Politische

Bereitschaften, and towards the end of the year patches bearing double Sig-Runes, hand-embroidered in silver bullion for officers and white or silver-gray cotton for other ranks, were issued to soldiers of the LAH. In June 1934 the SS PBs attached to Oberabschnitte Süd, Südwest and Mitte were authorized to wear runic 'SS 1', 'SS 2' and 'SS 3' patches respectively, with the numbers as large as the runes, and three months later non-commissioned ranks in the Leibstandarte and SS-VT were further distinguished by being allowed to use aluminum wire embroidery on their collar patches. In October, the piping on officers' patches was changed to the definitive plain aluminum cord, with the black/aluminum twist now being adopted by other ranks. The rest of the prewar period witnessed the introduction of machine-embroidered collar patches for the field uniform, death's heads and other designs for SS-TV and specialist units, and the adoption of the 'SS 1', 'SS 2' and 'SS 3' patches, this time with small numbers, by the 'Deutschland', 'Germania' and 'Der Führer' Standarten. Some collar patches were produced on metal bases with screw fittings at each corner, so they could be

easily removed from the tunic when it was being cleaned.

When army-pattern shoulder straps were introduced for the armed SS in March 1938, it was apparent that the wearing of dual rank badges on both the left collar patch (SS rank) and shoulder straps (army equivalent) was unnecessary. However, Himmler decreed that SS ranks should still be displayed. The situation was exacerbated at the outbreak of war, with the Leibstandarte, SS-VT and SS-TV being given specific roles alongside the Wehrmacht. The ordinary German soldier was bemused by the SS rank system, and was at a loss to know which SS men he was supposed to salute and whose orders he was obliged to obey. It therefore became absolutely essential, for practical and disciplinary reasons, that Waffen-SS rank badges should correspond to those in the armed forces and be easily recognized as such. Consequently, during the formation of the first SS field divisions in the autumn of 1939, it was decided that their personnel should not wear SS rank patches. Instead, they received matching collar patches with the runes or death's head on both sides. Their ranks were indicated solely by shoulder straps, in the army style. However, prewar Waffen-SS officers and men jealously retained their existing collar patches, showing their SS ranks.

The increased use of camouflage smocks, which covered the shoulder straps and, indeed, all insignia except the collar patches, led Himmler to rescind the matching collar patch order on 10 May 1940, and reintroduce the SS rank patch for all Waffen-SS members. At the same time, the need for security during the invasion of the Low Countries and France rendered obsolete

Authorized Collar Patches

Design	Period Used	Unit/Worn By
Blank	1933-45	Specialists/Departmental or HQ Staff/Units not yet allocated patches
SS	1933-45	LAH, then from 1940 all German and Germanic units not allocated other patches
SS/large 1	1934	SS PB 'Süd'
SS/large 2	1934	SS PB 'Südwest'
SS/large 3	1934	SS PB 'Mitte'
D	1934-37	Dachau Guard Battalion
K	1934-37	Concentration Camp Staff
Ü	1934-37	Dachau Training Camp
SS/T	1934-40	Bad Tölz Officers' School
SS/pick & shovel	1934-40	SS-VT Pioneer Battalion
SS/lightning bolt	1934-40	SS-VT Signals Battalion
SS/small 1	1935-40	'Deutschland'
SS/B	1935-40	Braunschweig Officers' School
SS/V	1935-40	Administration School
Vertical Death's Head	1936-40	Totenkopf Units
Vertical Death's Head/I-V	1936-37	SS-TV Battalion Staff
Vertical Death's Head/1-26	1936-40	SS-TV Companies
Vertical Death's Head/S	1936-40	SS-TV Medical Battalion
SS/small 2	1936-40	'Germania'
SS/S	1936/40	SS-VT Medical Battalion
SS/N	1936-40	'Nürnberg'
Vertical Death's Head/K	1937-40	Concentration Camp Staff
SS/small 3	1938-40	'Der Führer'
Police Litzen	1939-42	Police-Division
Police Litzen (woven)	1939-42	Police-Division
Horizontal Death's Head	1940-45	Totenkopf Units
Lion with axe	1941-43	Norwegian Legion
Lion with axe (metal)	1941-43	Norwegian Legion
Wolfsangel	1941-45	Dutch Legion/'Nederland'
Trifos	1941-45	'Nordwest'/Freikorps Danmark/Flemish Legion/'Langemarck'
Lyre	1941-45	Music School
Danish Flag	1942	Freikorps Danmark
Odal-Rune	1942-45	'Prinz Eugen'
Open Sonnenrad	1943-45	'Nordland'
SS (woven)	1943-45	All German and Germanic Units not allocated other patches
Horizontal Death's Head (woven)	1943-45	Totenkopf Units
Scimitar & Swastika	1943-45	'Handschar'
Lion Rampant	1943-45	14th (Ukrainian) Division
Swastika	1943-45	Latvian Legion/15th & 19th (Latvian) Divisions
Sun & Stars	1944-45	15th (Latvian) Division
E & Mailed Arm/Sword	1944-45	20th (Estonian) Division
Cornflower	1944-45	'Maria Theresa'
H	1944-45	'Hunyadi'
Crossed Rifles & Grenade	1944-45	Dirlewanger Brigade/36th Division
Three lions passant	1944-45	British Free Corps
Double-armed Swastika	1944-45	Non-SS Auxiliary Concentration Camp Guards
Flaming Grenade	1945	'Landstorm Nederland'
Flaming Grenade (metal)	1945	'Landstorm Nederland'

A large number of other embroidered collar patches exist which cannot be authenticated by contemporary photographic or documentary evidence. Many, if not all, are probably postwar fabrications. The table overleaf lists these 'alleged' SS collar patches.

ABOVE LEFT: SS-Gruppenführer Herbert Gille was the first Waffen-SS recipient of the Knight's Cross with Oakleaves, Swords and Diamonds. For this presentation photograph, taken on 20 April 1944, he wore a fine example of the General's Schirmmütze with aluminum piping, and the exquisitely hand-embroidered collar patches of his rank.

LEFT: SS assault troops in Russia, summer 1941. Collar patches were usually the only insignia visible while the camouflage smock was being worn.

RIGHT: Two shoulder straps piped in the brown Waffenfarbe of concentration-camp staff, alongside a selection of embroidered and woven horizontal death's head collar patches as worn from 1940 by Totenkopf personnel generally. The double-armed swastika patch dated from 1944 and denoted a non-SS concentration-camp guard.

all SS-VT and SS-TV collar patches bearing numerals or letters, which were ordered to be removed. For a short time during the western campaign, personnel in the SS-Verfügungsdivision wore no collar patches at all. From then on, the basic SS runes collar patch became standard for all German and Germanic Waffen-SS formations except Totenkopf units, whose members continued to wear the death's head, now produced in a horizontal version more suitable for use on the closed-neck field tunic. In August 1940, the black/aluminum twisted cord bordering other ranks' patches was abolished, leaving these patches unbordered for the rest of the war.

With the increasing recruitment of non-Germans into the Waffen-SS after 1940, Himmler became concerned about the use of the SS runes insignia by those not racially suitable for full SS membership, and he instructed that such recruits should wear some other form of badge on the right collar patch. The SS thereafter designed and issued a range of appropriate collar patches for its foreign units and, pending the distribution of these insignia, blank patches were often worn in new units as an interim measure. German SS officers and NCOs serving in foreign formations were still entitled to wear the SS runes collar patch and, as from July 1943, if they chose to identify with their men by wearing the distinctive unit patch, they were obliged to sport the SS runes embroidered below the left breast pocket instead. The latter insignia was identical to that worn by SS men in the German police.

The wearing of collar patches did not always conform to regulations. Matching patches and vertical death's heads, although prohibited in 1940, continued to be worn well into 1942, and officers often used other ranks' patches in the field, or removed the cording from their own patches. In 1943, machine-woven versions of the SS runes and horizontal death's head patches were produced, but the earlier embroidered examples were still being issued at the end of the war. Recruits under training often wore no collar patches at all.

The following table lists all SS-VT, SS-TV and Waffen-SS unit collar patches which have been confirmed by contemporary photographic or documentary evidence. They were produced in embroidered versions only, unless otherwise indicated.

Shoulder Straps

Members of the armed SS wore standard Allgemeine-SS shoulder straps on the right side only until 1935, when the earth-gray uniform was introduced. In July of that year, SS-VT officers were ordered to wear their Allgemeine-SS straps on both shoulders of the gray uniform. Other ranks received army-pattern straps made of plain earth-gray material, or earth-brown for SS-TV troops. In 1936 these enlisted men's shoulder straps were replaced first by a round-ended black version piped in black/aluminum twisted cord, then by an unpiped black type with pointed ends. None of these early straps identified the wearer's rank, as that was shown by his collar patches.

In March 1938, army-pattern shoulder straps with

Unauthorized Collar Patches

Design	Year Allegedly Produced	Unit/Intended for Wear by
SS/flaming grenade	Unknown	Probably Ordnance Related
SS/crossed lances	Unknown	Mounted Units
Viking Longship	1941	Norwegian Legion/'Wiking'
Closed Sonnenrad	1943	Danes in 'Nordland'
W	1944	Non-SS Auxiliary Concentration Camp Guards
Trident of Vladimir	1944	14th & 30th (Ukrainian) Divisions
SA Rune	1944	'Horst Wessel'
Goat's Head Helmet	1944	'Skanderbeg'
Sunburst	1944	'Kama'
Karst Flower	1944	24th (Italian) Division
Cross of St. George	1944	29th (Russian) Division
Fasces	1944	29th (Italian) Division
Sword & Wreath	1944	29th (Italian) Division
SS (on red patch)	1944	29th (Italian) Division
Cross of Burgundy	1945	'Wallonien'
Russian Orthodox Cross	1945	30th (Russian/Ukrainian) Division
Closed Sonnenrad	1945	33rd (Hungarian) Division
Sword of St. Joan	1945	'Charlemagne'
Crossed Grenades	1945	Dirlewanger Brigade/36th Division
Wolf's Head	1945	Crimean Tartars
Sword & Shield	1945	Caucasians
Tiger's Head	1945	Indian Legion

black underlay and gilt stars were issued to all armed SS officers, and NCOs began to wear aluminum lace, or Tresse, and white metal 'pips'. Rank was thereafter clearly indicated by the straps. From December 1939, officers sported colored Waffenfarbe piping between the aluminum braid and black underlay, and other ranks received their definitive Waffenfarbe-piped black straps with rounded ends.

A large number of unit identification insignia were worn on the shoulder straps. For officers, these numerals and ciphers were initially in gilt metal, then bronze after 1940. Other ranks had them embroidered directly onto their straps, or onto removable slip-on tabs from 1940. The table on the previous page lists the various identification badges known to have been used on Waffen-SS shoulder straps.

In October 1943, Himmler decided that Waffen-SS units and specialist personnel were adequately identified by collar patches, cuff titles and sleeve diamonds, and he forbade the wearing of shoulder-strap numerals and ciphers for the duration of the war. The only exception was the Leibstandarte-SS 'Adolf Hitler', whose members retained their LAH monograms.

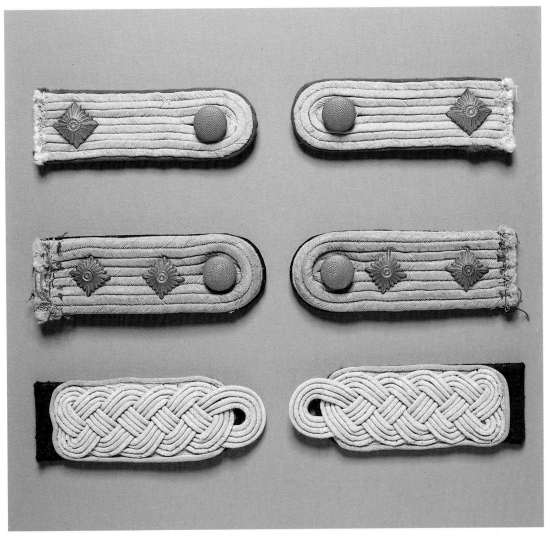

RIGHT: These pairs of Waffen-SS officers' shoulder straps indicate, from top to bottom: a Reconnaissance Obersturmführer, an Infantry Hauptsturmführer, and an RfSS Staff Sturmbannführer.

BELOW: An SS-Unterscharführer in Budapest, January 1945. He carries the Panzerfaust 60, a revolutionary and cheap anti-tank grenade-launcher which was used only once and then disposed of. Operating the Panzerfaust, or 'Armored Fist', was extremely simple, and it was very successfully handled by thousands of Volkssturm and Hitler Youth troops during the closing stages of the war.

Shoulder-strap Insignia

Badge	Unit
A	SS-VT Artillery Regiment
A (Gothic)	SS-VT Reconnaissance Battalion
AS/I	Artillery School I
AS/II	Artillery School II
Cogwheel	Technical Units
D	'Deutschland' Standarte
DF	'Der Führer' Standarte
E/Roman Numeral	Recruiting Offices
F1	SS-VT Anti-Aircraft MG Battalion
G	'Germania' Standarte
JS/B	Junkerschule Braunschweig
JS/T	Junkerschule Tölz
L	Motor Technical School
L (Gothic)	Training Establishments
LAH	Leibstandarte-SS 'Adolf Hitler'
Lyre	Bands
MS	Musikschule Braunschweig
N	'Nordland' Standarte
P (Gothic)	SS-VT Anti-Tank Battalion
Serpent	Veterinary Units
Serpent & Staff	Medical Units
SK/D	Dachau Garrison
SK/P	Prague Garrison
US/L	Unterführerschule Lauenburg
US/R	Unterführerschule Radolfzell
W	'Westland' Standarte
1 – 17	Totenkopf Standarten

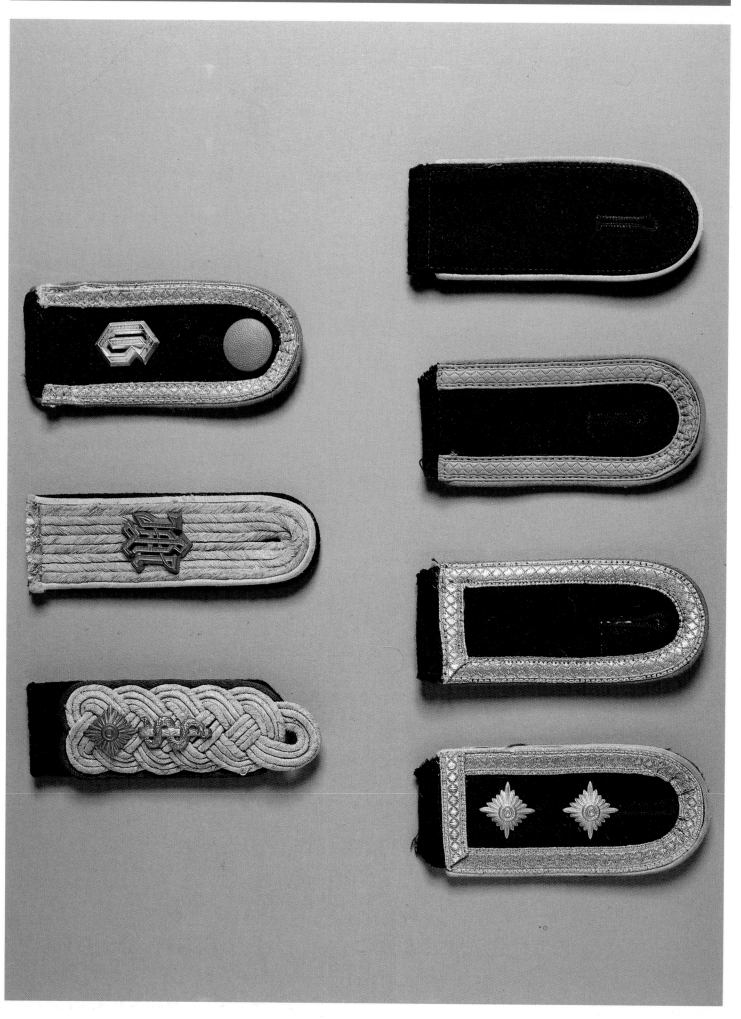

Cuff Titles

The cuff title, a woven black tape about 28mm in width and 49cm in length, which was worn on the lower left sleeve of the tunic and greatcoat, became one of the most distinctive features of SS uniform. Apart from identifying the unit of the wearer, it promoted a remarkable esprit de corps in the Waffen-SS.

All prewar regiments and most ancillary formations of the SS-VT and SS-TV had their own cuff titles, which were handed over as part and parcel of the clothing issue. Each man received four, one for each of his uniforms, and they were expected to last him nine months. These early cuff titles were embroidered in Gothic lettering with the exception of the Leibstandarte's 'Adolf Hitler' insignia, which featured the hand-written Sütterlin script officially reserved for the Führer's guards from 1936. On 1 September 1939, the Gothic 'SS' used on certain cuff titles was replaced by a runic version, and three months later all Gothic script was discontinued in favor of standard Latin lettering.

In May 1940, the cuff titles worn by ancillary Waffen-SS units, for example 'SS-Nachrichtensturmbann' and 'SS-Pioniersturmbann', were abolished as it was felt that they constituted a security risk. Regimental titles such as 'Deutschland' continued to be used, however, even after the introduction of divisional titles in 1942, and were worn by divisional personnel not entitled to regimental cuff titles. So a member of the signals battalion in the SS-Verfügungsdivision would wear the 'SS-Nachrichtensturmbann' title until May 1940, then no cuff title at all, and finally the 'Das Reich' title as from September 1942.

As the war progressed, cuff titles took on a new significance and were presented at solemn ceremonies during which unit commanders would remind recipients of the great honor being bestowed upon them and that they should do nothing to disgrace the names which their cuff titles bore. The exact criteria for awarding names and cuff titles is not known, but what is certain is that many SS divisions, like the 14th (Ukrainian) and 15th (Latvian), were never named, while some of those which were, such as 'Handschar' and 'Maria Theresa', never received cuff titles. Himmler apparently judged every application on its own merits, refusing some new units on the grounds that a cuff title had to be earned on the field of battle, and turning down others because they had been formed as a temporary wartime expedient from personnel considered racially unsuitable for SS membership.

LEFT: A selection of Waffen-SS shoulder straps. These denote, from top to bottom, left to right: a Signals Hauptscharführer, a Specialist Scharführer, a Mountain Troop Unterscharführer, an Infantry Schütze, a Medical Obersturmbannführer, a Signals Untersturmführer of the Leibstandarte, a panzer Unterscharführer of the 'Germania' regiment.

RIGHT: Woven SS cuff titles for, from top to bottom: staff of the Female SS Auxiliaries Training School at Oberehnheim, Civil Frontier Police (under the Sipo), Field Police, War Correspondents, Turkistani Volunteers (never worn).

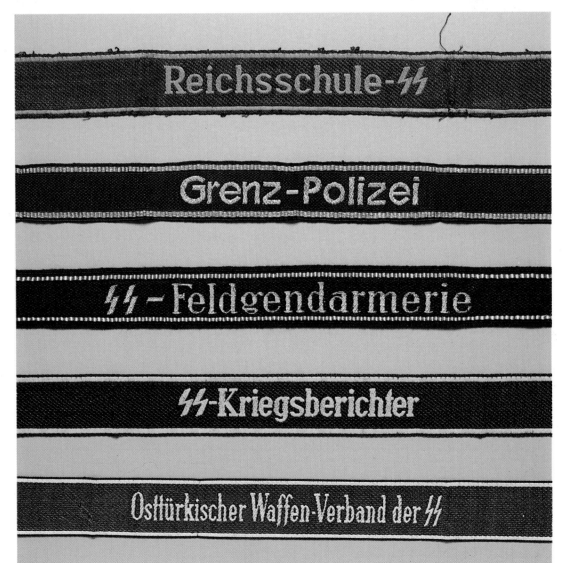

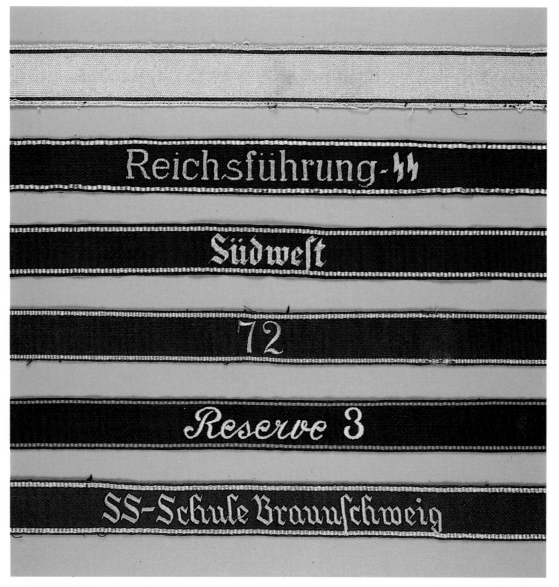

LEFT: A selection of cuff titles worn by, from top to bottom: the Reichsführer-SS and departmental chiefs; officers on the staff of the SS High Command; officers on the staff of Oberabschnitt Südwest; officers on the staff of the 72nd SS-Fuss-Standarte (Detmold); NCOs and men of the 3rd Sturm of a Reserve-Sturmbann; NCOs and men attached to the SS Officer School at Braunschweig (Brunswick).

RIGHT: A prewar shoulder strap of a junior officer of the SS-Totenkopf-standarte 3 'Thüringen' Division above cuff titles relating to, from top to bottom: the SS-Totenkopf-standarte 3 'Thüringen' Division; the SS-Totenkopfstandarte 1 'Oberbayern' Division; the SS-Panzergrenadier Regiment 6 'Theodor Eicke'; the 3rd SS-Panzer Division 'Totenkopf'.

Any Waffen-SS soldier transferring from one unit to another had to remove his old cuff title and replace it with that of his new unit. However, if the latter had not been awarded a cuff title, the man was permitted to continue to wear the title of his former unit. That explains why 'Adolf Hitler' and 'Der Führer' cuff titles featured among the officer cadre of the 24th SS Division in northern Italy at the end of the war, and why miscellaneous cuff titles were worn by SS paratroopers.

On occasion, two cuff titles could be worn together. Officer cadets being trained at Bad Tölz, for example, were initially allowed to wear the 'SS-Schule Tölz' cuff title above their own regimental or divisional titles, while war correspondents and military policemen often wore the 'SS-Kriegsberichter' and 'SS-Feldgendarmerie' titles below those of the regiment or division to which they were attached. The wearing of more than one cuff title in this fashion was forbidden in August 1943.

Cuff titles fell into the following four categories according to the method of their manufacture:

Hand-embroidered in aluminum wire or thread: Produced from 1933 until June 1942. For wear by all ranks until 1936, and thereafter by officers only.

Machine-embroidered in white or silver-gray cotton thread: The so-called 'RZM-style'. Produced from 1936-43 for wear by other ranks only.

Machine-woven in aluminum thread: Produced from 1939-43 for wear by officers only.

Machine-woven in flat gray cotton or silken thread: The so-called 'BEVO' pattern. Produced from 1943-45 for wear by all ranks.

It was not uncommon, however, for officers to use other ranks' cuff titles on their field tunics, or for NCOs to acquire officer-quality titles for wear on their dress uniforms. Moreover, old stocks of some early cuff titles continued to be worn long after they had been officially discontinued.

These categories are most important from a collector's point of view, for some cuff titles which appear on the market can readily be identified as reproductions simply because the date of introduction of the original does not correspond with the manufacturing technique of the copy. Cuff titles such as 'Florian Geyer', 'Hohenstaufen' and 'Reichsführer-SS', for example, which dated from 1943 and later, were all made in the BEVO

pattern and should not be encountered in the earlier RZM style. Similarly, Gothic script had been abandoned long before 1943, so it follows that Gothic lettering should not feature on BEVO cuff titles.

The table below lists all SS-VT, SS-TV and Waffen-SS cuff titles which have been confirmed by contemporary photographic or documentary evidence, together with their known manufacturing styles.

A few rare variant cuff titles are also known to have existed, but these were unofficial and even unique in some cases. Examples include Sepp Dietrich's wartime

'Adolf Hitler' cuff titles, which were embroidered in gold bullion, and the 'Wiking' and 'Wallonien' cuff titles hand-embroidered in Gothic script for wear by unit commanders Herbert Gille and Léon Degrelle respectively. A small number of unapproved localized cuff titles, such as the 'Narwa' and 'Estland' titles worn by some members of the 20th (Estonian) Division, are confirmed from photographs and were in all probability hand-embroidered. These are the exceptions which prove the general rules of cuff-title manufacture.

The following cuff titles were authorized during the

Waffen-SS Cuff Titles

Title	Year Introduced	Manufacturing Style
Adolf Hitler	1933	HE : RZM : MW : BEVO
Brandenburg	1937	HE : RZM
British Free Corps	1944	Manufacturing style cannot be discerned from the few surviving wartime photographs of members of this tiny unit. Probably hand-embroidered, as only a very small quantity was required.
Danmark	1943	BEVO
Das Reich	1942	RZM : MW : BEVO
Death's Head (insignia)	1938	HE : MW
Den Norske Legion	1941	HE
Der Führer	1938	HE : RZM : MW : BEVO
De Ruiter	1943	BEVO
Deutschland	1935	HE : RZM : MW
Elbe	1937	HE : RZM
E SS/TV	1939	MW
Florian Geyer	1944	BEVO
Freikorps Danmark	1941	RZM
Frundsberg	1943	BEVO
Frw. Legion Flandern	1941	RZM
Frw. Legion Nederland	1941	RZM
Frw. Legion Niederlande	1941	RZM : MW
Frw. Legion Norwegen	1941	RZM
General Seyffardt	1943	BEVO
Germania	1936	HE : RZM : MW : BEVO
Götz von Berlichingen	1943	BEVO
Hermann von Salza	1944	BEVO
Hitlerjugend	1943	BEVO
Hohenstaufen	1943	BEVO
Horst Wessel	1944	BEVO
Kdtr. Ü.L. Dachau	1935	HE
Kurt Eggers	1943	RZM : BEVO
Langemarck	1942	RZM : MW
Legion Niederlande	1941	HE
Legion Norwegen	1941	RZM
Michael Gaissmair	1944	BEVO
Nederland	1944	BEVO
Nordland	1940	HE : RZM : MW : BEVO
Nordwest	1941	RZM
Norge	1943	BEVO
Oberbayern	1937	HE : RZM : MW
Ostfriesland	1937	HE : RZM
Ostmark	1938	MW
Police Eagle (insignia)	1942	MW
Prinz Eugen	1942	RZM : MW : BEVO
Reichsführer-SS	1943	BEVO
Reichsführung-SS	1940	HE
Reichsschule-SS	1943	BEVO
Reinhard Heydrich	1942	RZM : MW : BEVO
Sachsen	1937	HE : RZM
Sanitätsabteilung	1936	HE : RZM
Skanderbeg	1944	BEVO
SS-Ärtzliche Akademie	1939	MW
SS-Feld-gendarmerie	1942	MW : BEVO
SS-Heimwehr Danzig	1939	RZM
SS-Inspektion	1936	HE
SS-KB-Abt	1941	RZM
SS-Kriegsberichter	1940	HE : RZM : BEVO
SS-Kriegs-berichter-Kp	1940	Unofficial Sütterlin script in chain-stitch embroidery
SS-Musikschule Braunschweig	1941	RZM
SS-Nach-richten-sturmbann	1937	HE : RZM
SS-Pionier-sturmbann	1937	HE : RZM
SS-Polizei-Division	1942	RZM : MW : BEVO
SS-Schule Braunschweig	1935	HE (Sütterlin until 1936) : RZM
SS-Schule Tölz	1934	HE : RZM
SS-Totenkopf-verbände	1937	MW
SS-Übungslager Dachau	1937	HE : RZM
SS-Unterführer-schule	1940	HE : RZM
SS-Verwaltungs-schule	1935	HE
Theodor Eicke	1943	BEVO
Thule	1942	RZM : MW
Thüringen	1937	HE : MW
Totenkopf	1942	RZM : MW : BEVO
Wallonien	1944	BEVO
W.B. Dachau	1935	HE
Westland	1940	HE : RZM : MW : BEVO
Wiking	1942	RZM : MW : BEVO

Key
HE – Hand-embroidered in aluminum wire or thread
RZM – Machine-embroidered in white or silver-gray cotton thread
MW – Machine-woven in aluminum thread
BEVO – Machine-woven in flat gray cotton or silken thread

war, but never issued for a variety of reasons: Artur Phleps, Charlemagne, Finnisches Frw. Bataillon der Waffen-SS, Hinrich Schuldt, 30 Januar, Landstorm Nederland, Latvija, Osttürkischer Waffen-Verband der SS, Woldemars Veiss. Most of these cuff titles existed on paper only. Examples of the 'Charlemagne', 'Landstorm Nederland' and 'Osttürkischer Waffen-Verband der SS' titles have appeared in a manufactured form, but these have yet to be authenticated by photographic or documentary evidence.

Arm Eagles

The eagle and swastika was established as the national emblem, or *Hoheitsabzeichen*, of the Third Reich on 7 March 1936. The insignia ultimately developed to incorporate a wide variety of forms, but the eagle invariably faced to its right when being used by State organizations such as the police and customs service, and to its left when being worn by the NSDAP and party formations like the SA and NSKK.

The first SS tunic eagles were sported by Sepp Dietrich and others as early as the summer of 1935, with the newly-introduced earth-gray uniform. The use of eagles on the right breast was restricted by law to the army, navy and air force, so members of the Leibstandarte and SS-VT took to wearing theirs on the left upper arm, in lieu of the gaudy Allgemeine-SS armband which was clearly unsuitable for field use. The pattern of sleeve eagle officially adopted by the armed SS in May 1936 was that introduced simultaneously for the

railroad police, with a right-facing eagle having dipping wings. It was discontinued after only two years, but was still being worn by some veterans in 1943.

The second and definitive pattern of SS national emblem, with a left-facing eagle and straight wings tapering to a point, was devised in 1938 and was eventually produced in several variations to become one of the most distinctive features of Waffen-SS uniform. The commonest manufacturing method was machine embroidery, in white or silver-gray cotton thread on black, and these RZM-style eagles came in the following three types, dependent upon period of production.

Between 1938 and 1941 the eagle had a pronounced square head; the 1942-43 version had a less pronounced curved head; and from 1944 a more shallow round head. Photographs confirm these types time and time again as period, rather than manufacturers', variations. The square-headed early eagle can regularly be seen in prewar shots and pictures taken during the western and Balkan blitzkriegs of 1940-41, while the round-headed insignia never features in these photographs. Conversely, the round-headed late-war eagle is consistently seen on camouflage drill tunics during the Normandy and Ardennes battles, with the early badge being conspicuous by its absence at that stage of the war.

In 1939, a BEVO machine-woven version of the SS sleeve eagle began to appear, in flat gray cotton or silken thread for other ranks and fine silver wire for officers. It was widely worn on all types of Waffen-SS uniform throughout the war, and was even used as a cap

RIGHT: SS-Obergruppenführer Wilhelm Koppe, Führer of Oberabschnitt Warthe, saluting his SS and police troops in 1943. Gau Posen was created on 26 October 1939, following the dissolution of Poland, and in January 1940 it was renamed Gau Wartheland after the River Warthe which ran through it. Koppe played an important role in the organization of SS forces in this new Reich territory, for which he received the rare Wartheland Gau Badge, clearly shown here on his left breast pocket. The Obersturmbannführer on the foreground wears the elongated Danzig Cross 1st Class, of which less than 100 were awarded for service in building up the prewar Nazi party in the Free City.

LEFT: By 1942 the SS had permeated every aspect of the German police system. A department known as the Hauptstelle der Hauptamt Ordnungspolizei was set up within the Reichsführung-SS to advise Himmler on all matters concerning the uniformed police and he, as Chef der Deutschen Polizei, made policy decisions regarding its operations and deployment. Police generals' distinctive green and gold collar patches were duly redesigned, with the traditional army style (above) being replaced by the new SS pattern, shown here for a Generalmajor der Polizei either side of a general's arm eagle. The SS membership runes remained silver for all ranks, including generals.

RIGHT: The police eagle ultimately appeared in many different forms and colors, to suit the vast array of uniforms worn by the Schutzpolizei, Gendarmerie, Verwaltungspolizei, Verkehrspolizei, Wasserschutz-polizei, Feuerschutzpolizei, Luftschutzpolizei and so on. At the end of 1942 the Waffen-SS Polizei-Division was accorded the honor of a unit cuff title, illustrated here in its BEVO-woven (above) and RZM-embroidered patterns.

badge by female SS auxiliaries. The BEVO eagle was also produced in tan-brown from 1943, for the tropical uniform. A few examples in green weave, allegedly for use on the spring side of the camouflage uniform, have made their way on to the market recently, but their authenticity has not yet been confirmed.

The SS arm eagle was also hand-embroidered in silver bullion for officers. Numerous slight variations existed, and a few had snaps attached to the rear so that they could readily be removed from the tunic when the latter was being cleaned. The bullion eagle was standard wear for all SS officers, although Sepp Dietrich again highlighted his unique status by having his insignia executed in gold wire.

In addition to the various regulation types of SS Hoheitsabzeichen, other eagles were sometimes worn on the left arm of the Waffen-SS tunic. A number of ex-army officers who transferred to the Waffen-SS, and foreigners who had previously served in Wehrmacht legions, wore the army breast-eagle on the sleeve, either to emphasize their origins or simply because the army eagle was more readily available to them. The use of army eagles was particularly common during the rapid expansion of the Waffen-SS in 1939-40, when SS eagles were in short supply and army-style Waffen-farbe piping and matching collar patches were the order of the day. A few SS-VT and SS-TV men on secondment to army units even wore the army eagle on the right breast while still sporting the SS eagle on the left arm. The Italian SS had their own version of the sleeve eagle, which was right-facing and clutched a fasces instead of a swastika, and between August 1942 and October 1944 the German police eagle in orange thread was worn by members of the SS-Feldgendarmerie.

Other Insignia

In addition to the insignia already mentioned, which were common to most Waffen-SS personnel, a number of other badges existed which merit only general coverage.

Members of the Polizei-Division wore police collar patches and headgear insignia until the beginning of 1942, when the unit was fully incorporated into the Waffen-SS. Thereafter, standard SS badges prevailed. Rather than completely re-decalling police helmets, however, the police eagle tended to be covered over with the runic shield, giving many SS-Polizei-Division helmets the appearance of having their Waffen-SS decals on the wrong way round.

A range of arm shields was created for foreign volunteers in the Waffen-SS, and generally took the form of machine-embroidered national flags on a black cloth ground measuring 60mm × 50mm. These were standardized in 1943, and most were produced by the Berlin firm of Tröltsch & Hanselmann. The shields were at first worn above the cuff title, and later beneath the SS arm eagle, and gradually replaced the army versions hitherto worn by many foreigners. The flags of Belgium, Denmark, Estonia, France, Great Britain, Holland, Latvia and Norway featured on these shields, while the badges for Albanian, Croatian, Finnish, Flemish and Ukrainian volunteers bore suitable heraldic motifs.

A series of trade badges to identify skills and specialties was designed in the shape of black cloth diamonds for wear on the lower left sleeve. Each badge was awarded after the successful completion of the relevant SS training course, and those who graduated from army schools were obliged to wear the army trade badge in lieu of the SS one. From October 1943, mountain troops sported a machine-embroidered edelweiss on the left side of the Bergmütze and on the right tunic sleeve, above the Honor Chevron of the Old Guard if the latter was also worn.

Uniformed female SS auxiliaries had a unique badge consisting of a black oval containing silver SS runes, which was sewn to the left breast pocket. Other civilian employees were given embroidered, woven or printed armbands bearing the words 'Waffen-SS' or 'Im Dienste der Waffen-SS' when in the war zone, and brassards featuring national colors were worn by young SS flak auxiliaries from the east. The latter were issued with a mixture of Luftwaffe and Hitler Youth uniform, and a printed triangular SS runes badge at the top of the left sleeve, in the manner of the HJ district triangle, was the only insignia which denoted their technical attachment to the Waffen-SS.

During World War II, Waffen-SS soldiers were eligible for the whole range of Nazi military decorations, including the Iron Cross, German Cross, War Merit Cross and so on. Participation in the Crimea, Demjansk and Kurland battles earned the appropriate campaign

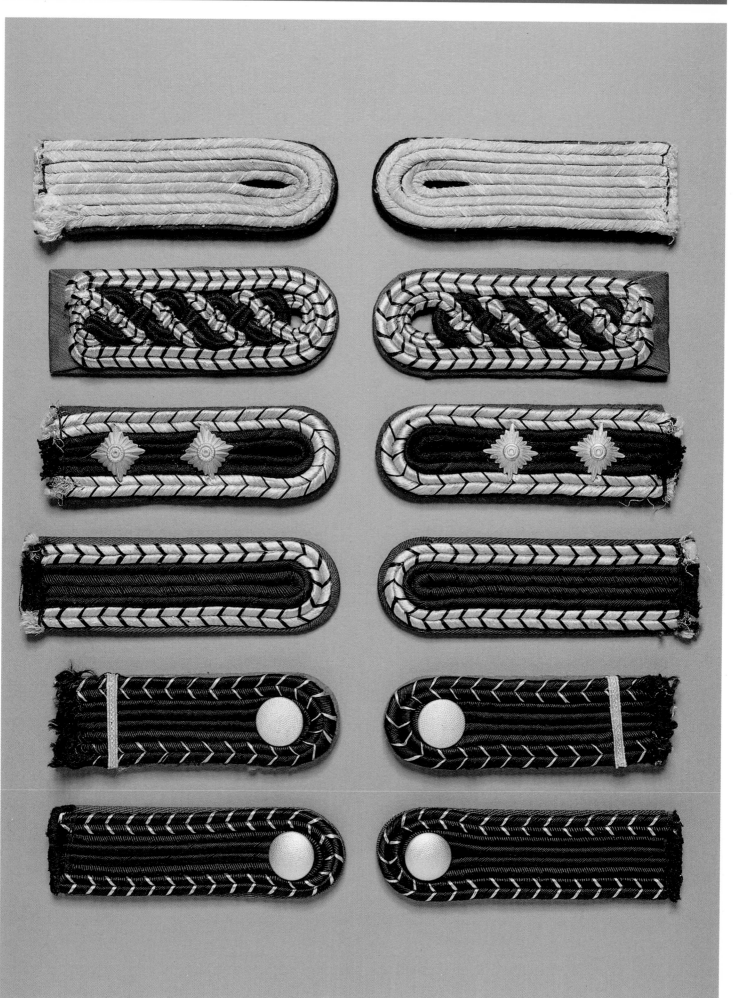

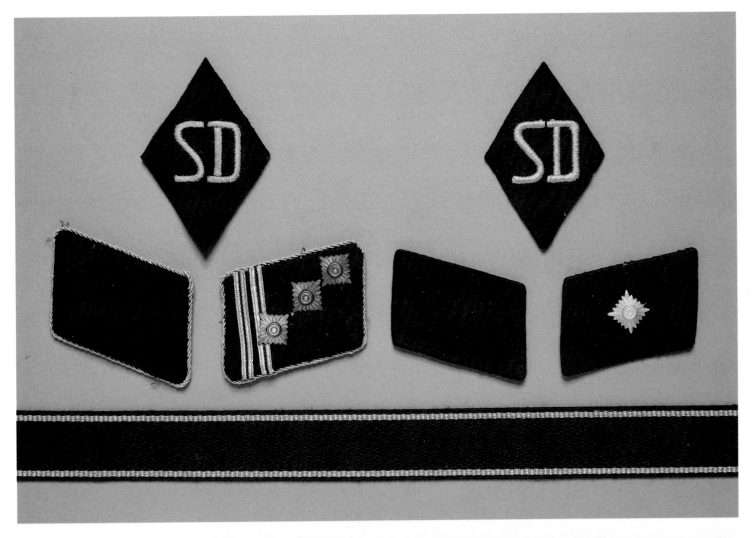

LEFT: In 1942, Sicherheitspolizei and SD personnel were allocated unique police-pattern shoulder straps in black and silver with green piping, to distinguish them from members of other SS and police formations. The pairs of straps shown denote, from top to bottom: Untersturmführer, Sturmscharführer, Hauptscharführer, Unterscharführer, Rottenführer, Sturmmann.

ABOVE: During the war, all members of the Sipo and SD operating in the occupied territories wore the SD uniform with its sleeve diamond, SS rank patch and blank right-hand collar patch. The blank cuff title was used by those on the staff of an SD Oberabschnitt.

RIGHT: Sipo and SD men with captured weapons in Poland, November 1939. The Sturmbannführer in the foreground commanded one of 16 Einsatzkommandos responsible for rounding up potential partisans following the invasion. The silver border to his SD sleeve diamond indicates Gestapo membership.

distinctions for men of the Leibstandarte, SS-Totenkopf-Division and VI Waffen-Armeekorps der SS, while troops of all units wore Infantry Assault, General Assault, Flak, Panzer Battle and Wound Badges, the Tank Destruction Award and the Close Combat Clasp. The SS Long Service Decorations of 1938 were superseded during the war by their Wehrmacht equivalents, since the Waffen-SS was regarded as an integral part of the armed forces. Even naval and Luftwaffe War and Qualification Badges could occasionally be seen on SS uniform, depending upon the wearer's service history.

Of all the German combat awards, only the Guerrilla Warfare Badge was singled out as being of specific relevance to the activities of the Waffen-SS, and for that reason it merits some detailed description. The increasing ferocity of the war waged against partisans in Russia, the Balkans and elsewhere during 1941-43 necessitated the creation of a new decoration to reward those who had been engaged upon it for a prolonged period. On 30 January 1944, Hitler instituted the *Bandenkampfabzeichen* and officially designated it a '*Kampfabzeichen der Waffen-SS und Polizei*', or 'Waffen-SS and Police Battle Badge', the only war

badge so described during the Third Reich. It came in three grades, bronze, silver and gold, for participation in 20, 50 and 100 combat days against guerrillas. Qualification for award was therefore very high, making the Bandenkampfabzeichen far more difficult to achieve than similar decorations like the Infantry Assault Badge. In fact, the Guerrilla Warfare Badge in Gold equated to winning the prized Close Combat Clasp in Gold twice.

The design of the Guerrilla Warfare Badge was based on that of the insignia of the Silesian Freikorps of 1919 and featured a wreath of oakleaves enclosing a sword with sunwheel swastika (representing the German forces) plunging into a hydra (the partisans). The hydra, a fabulous multi-headed sea serpent of Greek mythology, was famed as being almost impossible to destroy since its heads quickly grew again if they were cut off. The parallel with the partisan forces, which sprang up vigorously time and time again, is obvious. At the sword's point was a Totenkopf, which was doubly appropriate since it symbolized both the SS involvement in anti-partisan warfare and the deadly nature of the struggle.

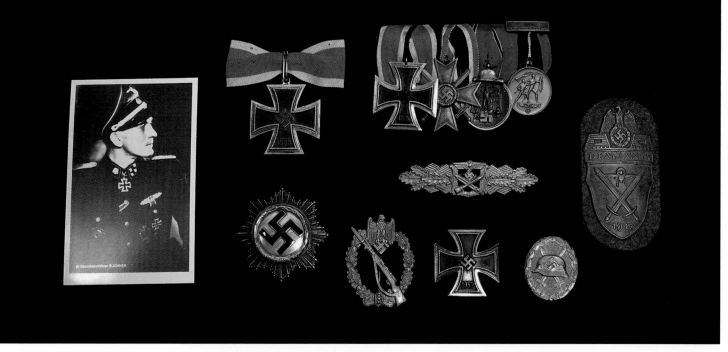

LEFT: After the invasion of Russia, various *ad hoc* anti-Soviet militias and home-guard units comprising mainly nationalist Balts and Ukrainians were consolidated into an auxiliary police force known as the Schutzmannschaft, or Schuma, with over 200 battalions, to assist the SS and Polizei in anti-partisan operations. Initially kitted out in modified surplus black Allgemeine-SS uniforms, they later received field-gray garb with their own rank badges and insignia incorporating the Schuma motto 'Loyal, Valiant, Obedient'. Branch of service colors were based on those of the German police. The armband, dating from August 1944, was worn with civilian clothes when on front-line duty with Sipo formations.

ABOVE: Sturmbannführer Hermann Buchner of the Totenkopf Division was one of the 'heroes' of the Waffen-SS, winning these awards before he was killed in action outside Warsaw in November 1944: Knight's Cross of the Iron Cross, German Cross in Gold, Iron Cross 1st and 2nd Classes, Close Combat Clasp in Gold, Wound Badge in Gold, Infantry Assault Badge in Silver, Demjansk Shield, War Merit Cross 2nd Class with Swords, Russian Front Medal, Czech Occupation Medal with Prague Castle Bar.

RIGHT: The Guerrilla Warfare Badge in Bronze.

THE GERMANIC-SS

Heinrich Himmler was possessed by his desire to improve the strength and racial composition of the German nation, and saw as the cornerstone of the Greater German Reich an SS organization with native branches in each of the occupied western territories. The NSDAP hierarchy had long agreed that all the areas which had formerly been part of the German (or Holy Roman) Empire, including Flanders and the Low Countries, should automatically be incorporated into the new Reich, with the mass of their populace eventually attaining full Reich citizenship. Himmler, however, went a step further, demanding that Germany should have the right to bring into its ranks the Germanic peoples of Norway and Denmark, states which had never been part of the Empire. The Reichsführer envisaged the ultimate creation of a new western Germanic State to be called Burgundia, grouping the Netherlands, Belgium and north-east France, which would be policed and governed solely by the SS according to the SS code. Burgundia would act as a buffer, protecting Germany proper from western invasion. The general aim was to attract all the Nordic blood of Europe into the SS, so that never again would the Germanic peoples come into mutual conflict.

Bli med oss nordover!

DEN NORSKE SKIJEGERBATALJON

PREVIOUS PAGES: Cossack volunteers under SS control on the Eastern Front.

LEFT: A recruiting poster calling upon volunteers to join the Norwegian-SS Ski Battalion. Raised in October 1942, this unit comprised 200 men under Obersturmführer Gust Jonassen, and served with the 'Nord' Division in Finland prior to being disbanded in May 1943.

RIGHT: Himmler visits Dachau. Note the Blood Order prominently displayed on his right breast.

To that end, Himmler established a replica of the German Allgemeine-SS in Flanders in September 1940. This Algemeene-SS Vlaanderen was joined two months later by the Dutch Nederlandsche-SS, and in May 1941 the Norges-SS was formed in Norway. Members of these units retained their own languages and customs, but there was to be no question of a Europe of semi-free pro-German states, each with its own independent SS formation loyal to its own political leader. From the start, Himmler told his western volunteers:

'Be certain of this. There will be in all Europe just one SS – the Germanic-SS under the command of the Reichsführer-SS. You can resist, but that is a matter of indifference to me for we will create it in any case. We do not ask you to turn against your country, nor to do anything repugnant to anyone proud of his country, who loves it and has his self-respect. Neither do we expect you to become Germans out of opportunism. What we do ask is that you subordinate your national ideal to a superior racial and historical ideal, that of the single and all-embracing Germanic Reich.'

Consequently, at the end of 1942, the western formations were removed from the influence of their own national collaborationist political leaders and amalgamated to become a new Germanic-SS under Himmler's direct orders. Their independence gone, they were now merely branches of a single organization and were re-titled Germaansche-SS in Vlaanderen, Germaansche-SS en Nederland, and Germanske-SS Norge. After the raising in April 1943 of the Danish Germansk Korpset, later called the Schalburg Corps, the Germanic-SS was complete, with a total active membership of almost 9000 men. Many of them had seen action in Russia, with the foreign volunteer legions of the Waffen-SS. All were duly kitted out with surplus black Allgemeine-SS uniforms imported from Germany, to which suitable national insignia were attached. Their primary wartime task was to support the local police by rooting out partisans, subversives and other anti-Nazi elements.

The uniform of the Germanic-SS in Flanders was virtually identical to that of the Allgemeine-SS. The only

NEDERLANDERS

VOOR UW EER EN GEWETEN OP !- TEGEN HET BOLSJEWISME DE WAFFEN ⚡⚡ ROEPT U !

LEFT: Inspired by a general call to arms against Communism, large numbers of Dutchmen enlisted in the Waffen-SS from 1940 onwards, serving in ever-growing self-contained formations which culminated in two full Dutch SS divisions, the 23rd 'Nederland' and 34th 'Landstorm Nederland'. No less than 22 members of Dutch Waffen-SS units won the Knight's Cross.

RIGHT: Another poster exhorting Norwegians to defend their eastern borders in the service of the SS Ski Battalion.

points of departure were that the peaked cap featured a large elongated silver swastika instead of the SS eagle, and a black diamond bearing the SS runes was worn on the left upper arm instead of the swastika arm-band. The diamond was piped in black/silver twisted cord for junior ranks and in silver bullion for officers. Rank insignia worn on the left collar patch was the same as that of the German SS, while the right collar patch was blank. On the lower left sleeve, a black-and-silver cuff title bore the legend 'SS-Vlaanderen', and the belt buckle featured the SS runes in a circle of oakleaves. Members of the Vlaanderen-Korps, which was in effect the Flemish SS reserve, wore a similar black uniform but were not entitled to sport either the peaked cap or arm diamond. They had forage caps with a silver swastika on the left side, and their cuff titles read 'Vlaanderen-Korps'. Moreover, their belt buckles had only a semi-circle of oakleaves around the runes.

Til vakt ved Nordens grense mot øst !

SS-SKIJEGERBATALJON NORGE

NORDMENN

KJEMP FOR NORGE

...d deg i Stortingsgata 12·OSLO

LEFT: This Norwegian poster depicts a Waffen-SS soldier as the direct descendant of a national hero, a theme common to recruiting drives in the Germanic countries. Note the 'Lion with Axe' collar patch of the Norwegian Legion.

RIGHT: Machine-embroidered cuff title and arm shield of the Flemish Legion. The 'Black Lion of Flanders' on a yellow background was also worn by soldiers of the 'Langemarck' assault brigade.

BELOW RIGHT: Members of the Germaansche-SS en Nederland on parade, 1943. Their uniform is clearly based on that of their counterparts in the Allgemeine-SS. The ranks used by the Germanic-SS in the Netherlands, including Hoofdschaarleider (Hauptscharführer), Onderstormleider (Untersturm-führer), were also copied directly from those of the German SS.

In civilian clothes, members of the Germanic-SS in Flanders could wear a circular lapel badge with a white swastika on a black background, while patron members, or *Beschermende Leden*, had their own diamond-shaped badge bearing SS runes and the letters 'BL'.

The nominal strength of the Flemish SS in June 1944 was 3500. However, 1600 of these were on active service with the Waffen-SS, 940 were with the NSKK and 500 were in the Vlaanderen-Korps, leaving only 460 regular Germanic-SS men in Flanders, of whom 100 were still probationers. By the end of the year, most of Belgium had been liberated. There was only one significant exception – the port of Antwerp, birthplace of the Flemish SS, which remained in German hands. The remnants of the Germaansche-SS in Vlaanderen were incorporated into a Security Corps of some 2500 assorted paramilitaries. A battalion of this corps fought alongside the German defenders of Antwerp in a battle which lasted throughout September-November 1944. It was one of the rare examples of western European collaborators being used to fight against the British and

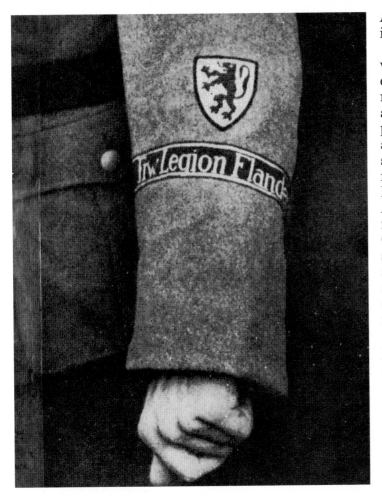

Americans, most of their colleagues seeing service only in Russia.

The uniform of the Germaansche-SS en Nederland was also black, with a regimental number on the right collar patch. A triangle bearing a silver Wolfsangel on a red-and-black background was worn on the left upper arm, and a silver metal Wolfsangel also appeared on the peaked cap in place of the SS eagle. On the right upper arm, the SS runes were worn on a black diamond, in silver bullion for officers and white cotton for lower ranks. All personnel wore blank cuff titles on the lower left sleeve. The 4000 patron members, or *Begunstigende Leden*, wore an oval lapel badge with the SS runes surmounting a swastika and the letters 'BL'. The Germaansche-SS en Nederland had, on paper, a strength of five regiments plus an SS-Police regiment, and supported its own journal, *Storm SS*. However, its active membership, nominally 3800 was in fact constantly depleted by voluntary enlistments into the more prestigious Waffen-SS.

The Norges-SS of 1941 wore a curious uniform comprising a field-gray open-necked tunic with a khaki shirt and black tie. Rank insignia was that of the *Rikshird*, (the Norwegian Nazi equivalent of the German SA) and the Rikshird's black armband with a sun cross and swords was worn on the left sleeve. Before the Norges-SS could complete even its basic training, however, Hitler invaded Russia and 85 per cent of its membership immediately volunteered for service with the Norwegian Legion of the Waffen-SS. The remainder

LEFT: Arm shields designed for Waffen-SS units staffed by volunteers from Holland, Norway, Italy (never worn), Denmark, Estonia, Latvia and Croatia.

RIGHT: Troops of the SS-Freiwilligen Legion 'Niederlande' wearing Dutch-made arm shields and cuff titles in August 1941.

BELOW: A selection of Waffen-SS collar patches relating to foreigners and others deemed unworthy of the SS runes. Some of these insignia have never been authenticated by wartime photographs or documentary evidence. A large number of fakes are now in circulation, and these are frequently offered for sale as having been 'found unissued in the Dachau clothing stores in 1945'.

LEFT: The Germanic Proficiency Rune in Bronze, less than ten of which are still known to survive. The small badge above was worn by Patron Members, or Beschermende Leden, of the Germanic-SS in Flanders.

BELOW: Cuff titles authorized for Waffen-SS units composed of a mixture of German, Germanic and Volksdeutsche personnel.

RIGHT: In February 1944, recruits for the Französische SS-Freiwilligen Grenadier Regiment were sworn in. They formed the nucleus of the 7000-strong French SS division 'Charlemagne', which was destroyed in eastern Germany at the end of the war.

Prinz Eugen

Frundsberg

Horst Wessel

Wiking

Norge

Hermann von Salza

went into a police company, which took part in the siege of Leningrad. In July 1942, many veterans returned from the east to form the new Germanske-SS Norge, which abandoned all Rikshird associations. A new oath of allegiance was taken to Hitler, and the German-inspired motto 'Min aere er troskap' ('My Honor is Loyalty') was adopted. The uniform of the Germanske-SS Norge was all black except for a brown shirt. It comprised a ski-cap (peaked caps were never worn by the Norwegian SS), an open-necked tunic, ski trousers and mountain boots. An eagle holding a sun cross in silver and black was worn on the left sleeve above a cuff title bearing the legend 'Germanske-SS Norge'. Rank insignia appeared on the left collar patch with a silver sunwheel swastika on the right patch. SS runes on a black diamond were sported on the right upper arm.

No Germanic-SS unit in Norway attained sufficient size to be regarded as a Standarte. The largest that could be mustered was a Stormbann or battalion, of which there were 12 in various parts of the country. Most were consistently under strength. The concept of patron members was introduced into Norway as in the other Germanic countries, and these so-called *Stottende Medlemner* were entitled to wear a small oval badge in black enamel, with silver SS runes and the letters 'SM'. Official figures published in *Germaneren*, the Norwegian SS newspaper, gave the strength of the Germanic-SS in Norway as 1250 in September 1944. Of these, 330 were on combat duty with the Waffen-SS and 760 were in police units, leaving only 160 Norwegians in the active Germanic-SS. At the same time, there were 3500 patron members.

The Danish Germanic Corps, or Germansk Korpset, was formed in 1943 from Russian-front veterans and shortly thereafter was renamed the Schalburg Corps in memory of their former leader who had been killed at Demjansk. The unit adopted a black uniform virtually identical to that of the Allgemeine-SS, with similar rank insignia, although the nomenclature used was that of the Danish police. The main points of departure were that the SS cap eagle was replaced by a winged sunwheel swastika, and a sunwheel swastika also appeared on the right collar patch and on the belt buckle. A Danish heraldic shield, comprising three blue lions on a yellow field with red hearts, was worn on the upper left arm above a cuff title bearing the word 'Schalburg'. On ceremonial guard duty, a highly-polished black German steel helmet was worn with a large white sunwheel swastika on the right side. The Schalburg Corps adopted the same techniques as the partisan groups which it fought, and responded to each resistance assassination with one of its own. A so-called Schalburg Cross, bearing the Corps motto 'Troskab vor Aere' ('Our Honor is Loyalty') was instituted late in the war, with one posthumous award being made.

In addition to the Germanic-SS formations permanently based in Flanders, Holland, Norway and Denmark, the Allgemeine-SS established its own *Germanische Sturmbanne* or Germanic battalions in the areas of the Reich where there were large concentrations of workers imported from the Nordic countries. These foreigners numbered several hundred thousand by the end of 1942, and posed a major problem for German internal security. To assist in their control, Flemish and Dutch SS officers and men, most of them fresh from front-line service in the east, were employed by German firms to engage in a propaganda campaign in the factories. They succeeded in persuading such large

numbers of their compatriots to join the local Allgemeine-SS that seven Germanic battalions were set up in the major industrial cities of Berlin, Braunschweig, Dresden, Düsseldorf, Hamburg, Nürnberg and Stuttgart. Uniforms were supplied by the Allgemeine-SS and comprised the standard black outfit, minus the tunic. Insignia was worn on the shirt, in the manner of the old SS traditional uniform. Membership peaked at around 7000 at the end of 1944, with the sole function of policing foreign workers in Germany.

Initially, SS personnel from Flanders, Holland, Norway and Denmark were entitled to compete for and wear the paramilitary sports badges awarded by their domestic pro-Nazi parties. However, the formation of the Germanic-SS at the end of 1942 all but severed the links with home and consequently a new all-embracing sports award was called for. On 15 July 1943, regulations introduced just such a badge for the Germanic-SS. It was to take the form of two sig-runes, long the emblem of the German SS, superimposed over a sunwheel swastika, which was associated with pro-Nazi parties across Europe as well as with the Waffen-SS Wiking and Nordland divisions in which many west-

European volunteers were serving. The design was therefore representative of the union between the German SS and the Germanic-SS. Approved and instituted by Himmler on 1 August 1943, the award was named the *Germanische Leistungsrune*, or Germanic Proficiency Rune. It came in two grades, bronze and silver, the badges differing only in the color of the sunwheel. The tests leading to an award of the badge were on a par with those undergone by Germans in the SS to qualify for the German National Sports Badge and the SA Military Sports Badge. They included running, jumping, swimming, rope climbing, throwing the hammer, shooting, completing an assault course, map reading, distance judging, observation, camouflage, first aid, signaling, verbal reporting and report writing. There were also written and oral examinations on National Socialist theories. Training requirements meant that at least 120 hours practise had to be completed every six months, and tests had to be passed annually in order to retain the badge.

The first tests and examinations took place in January 1944 at the training school of the Dutch SS at Avegoor near Arnhem. Over 2000 members of the

LEFT: In November 1944, the SS assumed control of the German Army's 1st and 2nd Cossack Cavalry Divisions.

ABOVE: The oval badge for Patron Members, or Stottende Medlemner of the Germanic-SS in Norway (left), was akin to the civil lapel pin worn by German SS members when out of uniform.

ABOVE RIGHT: Gross, Dietrich, Jungclaus and Degrelle at a parade to celebrate the safe return of the latter's Belgian SS Brigade.

RIGHT: Nikolajs Galdins, a Latvian, wearing the Knight's Cross. Note the swastika collar patch of the 15th and 19th SS divisions.

LEFT: SS-Gruppenführer Reinhard Heydrich, Chief of the Security Police and SD, in 1937.

Germanic-SS presented themselves, but only 95 passed. They were decorated with the badge (18 silver and 77 bronze) by Himmler on 1 February. The following June, 20 Danes received the badge at a ceremony at their training center at Hovelte, and in August 25 members of the Germanic-SS in Norway were similarly decorated. The Allied invasion of western Europe undoubtedly prevented more widespread distribution, and it is believed that total awards numbered less than 200. Many badges were destroyed by their recipients at the end of the war, for obvious reasons.

The Germanic Proficiency Rune was convex in form, and measured 46mm in diameter. The sunwheel was of copper-plated zinc with an olive-bronze or silver wash, while the sig-runes were black enameled tombakbronze with silver-plated edges. The sig-runes were secured to the sunwheel by four round tombak pins bent over at the rear. The reverse had a typically 'bubbled' appearance, and was unmarked. The pin bar was wide and flat. Since intended distribution was strictly limited, it is most probable that all Germanic Proficiency Runes were produced at a single source. Unfortunately, due to the absence of makers' marks, that source remains a mystery. However, it is more than likely that the badge was made 'in-house' by one of the many SS economic enterprises. It has been widely faked, with most copies being made from a bright alloy, with soldered runes and RZM marks. A completely bogus 'Germanic Proficiency Rune in Gold' has even appeared on the memorabilia market in recent years.

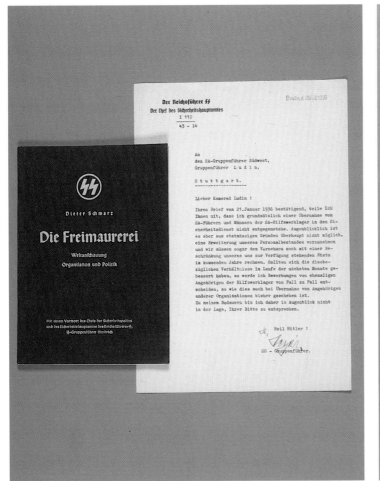

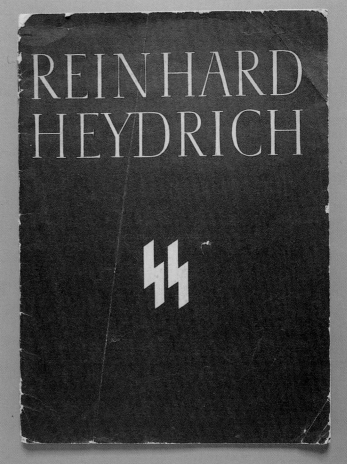

ABOVE: An SS anti-Freemasonry publication, with a foreword by Heydrich, alongside correspondence signed by Heydrich, Schwarz and Pohl.

ABOVE RIGHT: On 27 May 1942, while acting as Deputy Reichsprotektor of Bohemia and Moravia, Heydrich war blown up by Czech agents in Prague and died a week later. This memorial book was subsequently produced by the SS in his honor.

RIGHT: A commemorative stamp showing Heydrich's death mask, alongside another portraying a Waffen-SS mortar crew in action.

INDEX

Page numbers in *italics* refer to illustrations.

Abschnitte (districts) 18, 66, 125
Ahnenerde, ancestral research
   organization 29
Allgemeine-SS 18, 22-63, 145
   conditions of service 27, 50
   daggers of 52
   economic role of 29
   flags and banners of 60
   non-German nationals in 154
   ranks and titles 50
   recruitment for 25, 27, 29
   regimental organization 22
   role and aims of 22, 25, 27, 29
   uniforms and regalia 29, 32-47,
     92, 121, 122, 124
Ardennes offensive 76, *76,* 113, *113,*
   119, 135
Arnhem operation of 76, *99*
Austria, occupation of 29
awards and decorations *95, 109,*
   135, 137, 140 153
   Blood Order (NSDAP) *14-15,* 40,
     145
   German Cross 137, 141
   Guerrilla Warfare Badge 140, *141*
   Honor Chevron for Old Guard 41,
     41, 43
   Iron Cross *93,* 137
     Knight's Cross of *66, 109, 126,*
     141, *146, 155*
   Sports awards (Germanic
     Proficiency Rune) *152,* 154-5
   SS Death's Head Rings 32, 35,
     57-8, *58*
   see also badges and insignia

Badges and insignia 121-2, 124-6,
   132, 135, 137-40
   arm eagles *68,* 135-6
   arm shields 137
   armbands 92, *120*
   belts and buckles 41, *48-9, 109,*
     146
   Blood Order *see under* awards
     and decorations
   cap badges 32, *32,* 42, 43
   cloth badges *120,* 121-2
   cuff titles *see main entry*
   Hoheitabzeichen 41
   Honor Chevron for Old Guard *see*
     under awards and decorations
   Golden Party Badge *14-15,* 40
   metal badges 121
   Pilot-Observer Badge 24
   production of badges 121-2
   specialist trade badges *43,* 137
   Tag der Arbeit badge *53*
   Waffenfarbe 124-5, 128
   see also awards and decorating;
     collar patches; daggers;
     shoulder straps
Bandfabrik Ewald Vorsteher (BEVO)
   company 122, 124, 132, 134,
   135-6
Berchtold, Josef 11, 12
Bewaffnete-SS 18
Bormann, Martin *24*
Bouhler, SS-Gruppenführer Philipp
   53

Brandt, SS-Sturmbannführer
   Wilhelm 99
Brückner, Wilhelm *54*
Buchner, Sturmbannführer Hermann
   141
Büchner, Reichszeugmeister
   Richard 122

Collar patches *34,* 38, *44, 68, 78,*
   124, 125-8, *126,* 136, 137, 149,
   151, 153, *155*
concentration camps 18, 29, *90*
   Belsen 82
   Dachau *28, 30,* 81, 124, *145*
   manufacturing enterprises in 29,
     30-31, 81, 119, 124
   SS guards for (*Wachverbände*) 66,
     97
cuff titles 38, 41, *68, 95,* 124, 131-2,
   131-2, 134-5, 149, *151-2*
Czechoslovakia, occupation of 29

Daggers 52, *52-3,* 54
   'chained dagger' *52,* 54, 55
   manufacture of 52
   Röhm SS Honor Dagger 54, 56
   SS Dagger *Dienstdolch* 52
   for Waffen-SS 54
Daluege, Kurt 12, 41
Darré, SS Obergruppenführer
   Richard Walther *44*
Degrelle, Léon 134
Denmark, Schalburg Corps 145, 153
Deschler company 32, 121
'Deutschland Erwache' motto 60
Diebitsch, SS-Oberführer, Prof.
   Doctor Karl 42, 54
Dietrich, Oberstgruppenführer Sepp
   64-5, 66, *67-8,* 76, *76,* 118, 134,
   135, 136
Drexler, Anton 8
Dutch SS 35

East Front war *73,* 73-4, *75,* 76, *79,*
   116, 119, *119, 127,* 142-3, 153
Eicke, SS-Obergruppenführer
   Theodor 66, *66*
Eickhorn, Karl, company 52, 54

Fahnen-Hoffmann, company 63
flags and banners *6-7, 10, 12,* 58, 60,
   63
   battalion flags 63
   Blood Banner 58, 60
   command flags 63
   Deutschland Erwache flag 60, 63
   regimental standards 60
   vehicle pennants *62*
FM (*Fordernde Mitglieder*)
   organization 18
   FM-Zeitschrift magazine *17-18*
France,
   SS Division 'Charlemagne' *153*
   see also West Front war
Frederick William I, King 32
Freikorps 8, *9,* 11, *13,* 32, 35, 36, 140

Gahr, Otto, company 57
German Workers' Party 8
Germanic-SS 44, 142-55
   in Denmark 145, 153, 155
   in Flanders 145-6, 148
   in Netherlands 145, 148, *148-9,*
     154
   in Norway 145, 149, 153, 155
Gille, Herbert 134
Goebbels, Josef 12, *53*

Göring, Hermann 11
Graf, Ulrich 11
Grimminger, SS-Standartenführer
   Jakob 58, 60, *60*
Günsche, Otto *49*

Haas, Prof. Hans 87
Hammerfahr, Gottlieb, company 52
Hausser, Paul 66, 70, 73, 99, 105
headgear 36, 42, 43, 51, 79, 82-91,
   126, 137
   'crusher' cap *75,* 88-9, *89*
   fez *78-9,* 91
   field cap *45, 51,* 82, *82,* 84, 89, 90,
     90, 91
   peaked cap 42, *42,* 89
   schirmmütze 42, 86, 89, 91
   services cap *86-7,* 90
   shako 85
   steel helmuts *33,* 36, 82, 84, *84,*
     86-7, 87, *89,* 90=91
   for Waffen-SS 82, 84, 87, 89-91,
     102, 110, 115
Heck, Walter 35
Heiden, Erhard 12
Herder, Richard 52
Hess, Rudolf *11,* 28, 35, *64-5*
Heydrich, Reinhard *8,* 44, *154,* 157
Himmler, Heinrich *8,* 11, *13, 14-15,*
   28, 58, *64-5, 123,* 145
   Chief of Police 25, 136
   and Germanic-SS 144-5, 154, 155
   as *Reichführer der SS* 12, 13, 14,
     29, 32, 50, 63, 81
   security chief of NSDAP 12
   and uniforms and regalia 24, 32,
     34, 52, 54-8 *passim,* 92, 124,
     126, 128, 131
   and Volksturm 25
Hindenburg, President Field Marshal
   Paul von 13
Hitler, Adolf *22-4,* 35, *44, 54,* 56, *60,*
   64-5, 73, *116,* 140
   assassination attempt on 29
   becomes Chancellor 14
   and NSDAP 8, 11, 38, 41
   in Nurnberg *6-7, 10-11,* 60
   and SS 14, 22, *38, 49,* 50, *51, 56,*
     66, 68, 73-4, 76
   and war in the West 76
Hitler Youth 25, 41, *53*
Hoffmann, Heinrich *67*
Hoffstätter, Ferdinand, company 35

Italian army, source of uniforms 113,
   115
Italian SS 91, 97, 136

Jacobs & Company 52

Kempf, Generalmajor 99
Kharkov, assault on 54, 73, 113
Klaas, Robert 52
Koppe, SS-Obergruppenführer
   Wilhelm *135*
Krasse, SS-Standartenführer
   HugoGottfried *49*
Krause, Karl Wilhelm *121*
Kripo (*Kriminelpolizei*) 18
Kursk, battles at 74

Litzmann, General Karl *23*
Luftwaffe, and parachutists 113-14
Lutze, Viktor 15

Manteuffel, Freiherr von *9*

Meyer, SS-Oberstümbannfuhrer Kurt
   112
Mohnke, SS-Hauptsturmführer
   Wilhelm *23*
Muller, Paul 56
Munich *Putsch,* 1923 11, 35, 36, 58,
   60
Mussolini, Benito 113, 114

Netherlands, Germanic-SS in 145-6,
   146, 148, *148-9,* 154
'Night of the Long Knives', 1934 14,
   54, 66
Nordic racial studies 29, 144
Norway, Germanic-SS in 145, 149,
   153, 155
NSDAP (*Nationalsozialistische
   Deutsche Arbeiterpartei*) 144
   foundation and early years of 8,
     10, 11, 12-13
   uniforms and badges of 35, 38,
     60, 121, 135

Oberabschnitte (regions) 18, 63
Overhoff company 41

Pack, Ernst & Söhne 52
Party newspaper 12, *17*
Pohl, SS-Obergruppenführer Oswald
   46
police 18, 22, 25, 50, 54, 55, 58, 70,
   139
   SS-Polizeidivision 70, *73, 87,* 92,
     137
Prutzmann, Hans *8*

Reichsarbeitsdienst 27
Reichswehr 8, 11, 14, 29, 32, 66
   Sixth Army 73
Reinhardt, C. Bertram 52
Ribbentrop, Joachim von 56
Riefenstahl, Leni 92
RKFVD (*Reichskommissariat für die
   Festigung des deutschen
   Volkstums*) 27
Röhm, Ernst 8, *8-10,* 11, 13, *13-15,*
   14, 54, *123*
Rossbach, Gerhard 36
Runes symbols *34-5,* 52, 54, 55, 57,
   84, 87, 91, 122, 128
   Hagall-Rune *35,* 57
   Sig Runes *24, 27, 29,* 35, 57, 125,
     154
RZM (*Reichszeugmeisterei*) 82, 84,
   90, 121, 122, 124, 134, 135

SA (*Sturmabteilungen*) 8, 11, 12, 50
   Night of the Long Knives *see main
     entry*
   uniform 36, 38, *40,* 42
Saalschutz (Hall Guard) 8
Saloman, Franz von *11*
Sauberzweig, SS-Brigadeführer Karl
   81
Schaub, Julius *54*
Schirach, Baldur von *54*
Schumann, Heinrich 92
Schreck, Julius 11, *11,* 91
Schutzmannschaft auxiliary police
   force 141
Schwartz, SS-Oberstgruppenführer
   Franz Xaver 39, 54
Schwarze Korps, Das, journal *17*
SD (*Sicherheitsdienst*) 18, *19,* 96
   daggers for 54
shoulder straps 41, 45, *48,* 124, *125,*
   126, *127,* 128-9, *129-30, 133, 138*

Skorzeny, SS-Sturmbannführer Otto 113, 114, *114*
SS (*Schutzstaffel der NSDAP*) 14
  armbands for 36, *36*
  awards for 57
    Death's Head Ring *see under main entry* awards and decorations
  cap insignia 32, *33*
  daggers for 52, 54, 56
  documents of *16, 25, 26*
  flags and banners 58, 60, 63
    Reiterstandarten 60
    Sturmbannfahne 63
  independent of SA 14
  marriage ceremonies *26-8*
  organization *see main heading* SS organization *below*
  origins and growth 11-13, *13,* 14
  patron members of 17, 18, 29
  prime role of 22, 68, 70
  ranks and titles 48, 50
  SS formations *see main entry* SS formations *below*
  standard bearers 63
    gorget for *58,* 63, *63*
  uniforms for 35, 36-9, *38,* 41-5, *58*
  swords for 35-6
SS formations,
  Sixth SS-Panzer Army 76
  Panzer Corps 73, 74
    DIVISIONS
    'Florian Geyer' 76
    Gebirgs Division 'Nord' *125*
    'Handschar' 74, *78-9*
    'Hitler Jugend' 74, *74,* 113, *118*
    Kavallerie Division 73
    'Maria Theresa' 76, 131
    Polizei Division 70, *73, 87,* 92, 137
    'Prinz Eugen' 74
    'Reichsfuhrer-SS' 76, 115
    Totenkopf Division 70, *70-72,* 73, 74, 76, 92, 140
    OTHER FORMATIONS
    Fallsschirmjager Battalions 113, 114, 132
    Reiterstandarten 55, 60, 63
    Sonderkommando Zossen *51*
    Totenkopfverbände 66, 68, 70, 92, 125, 126, 128, 131, 136
    Wachverbände 66, 87
SS organization,
  Bekleidungswerke 81, 119
  Fúhrershauptamt 14, 124
  Hauptamt 14, 63, 124
  Hauptamt Personlicher Stab 14, 97, 124
  Hauptamt SS-Gericht 18
  Personalhauptamt 18
  Politische Bereitschaften 66, 125
  Rasse- und Siedlungshauptamt 18, 44
  Reichsarbeitsdienst 27
  Reichskommissariat für die Festigung des Deutschen Volkstums 27
  Reichssicherheitshauptamt 18
  Volksdeutsche Mittelstelle 29
  Wirtschafts- und Verwaltungshauptamt 18, 124
SS standardbearers 63
  Kornet (gorget) for *58,* 63, *63*
SS *Wachverbände* 66, 87
Staatsschützkorps (State Protection Corps), proposed 25
Stabswache bodyguard 11, 36
Stalingrad, battle at 73
Steiner, SS-Gruppenführer Felix 70, 73
Stosstrupp Adolf Hitler 11, 32, 36, *36,* 41

Strasser, Gregor *11*
swastika symbols 35, 36, *36,* 60, 135, 154
swords *55,* 55-6
  birthday swords 56
  Ehrendegen 55
  police swords *57*
  SS-Reichführer's Sword of Honor *55*

Totenkopf insignia *20-21,* 32, *32-3,* 42, 43, 54, 57-8, 66, 82, 87, 110, 121, 124, 128, 140

Uniforms and regalia *14-15,* 18, *22, 102-3, 116-19,* 135
  of Allgemeine-SS 29, 32-47
  black uniform *13,* 42-4, *44, 45,* 89, 92, *92,* 145, 154
  camouflage clothing *98,* 99, *100-101,* 101, *104-7,* 105, 110, 113, *118-19,* 124, 126, 136
  field gray uniform 44, 45, *46-7,* 54, *70,* 89, 114
  of Germanic-SS 145-6, 148-9
  made in concentration camps 29, 81
  police uniform *103*
  prices of 43
  protective clothing 115, 117, 119
  tradition uniform 35, 38, 41
  tropical clothing 115, 136
  of Waffen-SS 45, *45,* 81, 92, 94, 97, 110, *110-11,* 113-14, 115

Völkischer Beobachter 12
Volkssturm (Home Guard) 25

Waffen-SS 25, 64-141
  conditions of service 50
  documents *80*
  headgear for *see under main heading*
  non-German nationals in 79, 81, 91, 128, 137, 145, 146, 149
  war casualties 76, 79
Waffen-SS formations,
  Panzer-Korps 73, 74
    DIVISIONS
    14th (Ukrainian) 131
    15th (Latvian) 131
    20th (Estonian) 134
    23rd 'Nederland' 146
    24th 97, 132
    29th 97
    34th 'Landstorm Nederland' 146
    'Das Reich' 70. 73, 74, *101,* 131, 135
    'Gotz von Berlichingen' 74
    'Hitlerjugend' 74, 115
    'Hohenstaufen' 73, 74, 76
    'Frundsberg' 73, 74, 76
    'Prinz Eugen' 115
    'Reichsfuhrer-SS' 115
    'Nordland' 154
    'Wiking' 70, *73,* 74, 76, 115, 134, 154
    REGIMENTS AND OTHER UNITS
    'Der Fuhrer' Standarte 68, 125
    'Germania' Standarte 68, 70, 125
    Junkerschulen 56
    Leibstandarte 'Adolf Hitler' *20-23, 22, 50, 56, 58, 61, 64-5,* 66, 68, *69,* 70, 73, 74, 84, 87, 92, *92,* 97, *112,* 113, 115, *116,* 122, 125, 126, 128, 131, 135, 140
    SS-Heimwehr 68, 70

Verfügungstruppe 66, 99
VT Standarte 'Deutschland' *50,* 68, 70, 87, 92, 97, 110, 122, 125, 126, 128, 136
Wagner, Gauleiter Adolf 60
Wehrmacht 68, 124
Weimar Republic, political unrest in 13
Weitzel, SS-Obergruppenführer Fritz 54
West Front war *70,* 74, *74-6,* 76, 113, *113,* 126, 135, 148
Wevelsburg castle 58
Wisch, Hauptsturmführer Theodor *56, 69,* 76
Witt, Fritz (Panzer officer) 76, 118
Wolff, SS-Obergruppenführer Karl *8, 28,* 97
Wünsche, Max (Panzer officer) *76*

Acknowledgments

The author and publisher would like to thank Judith Millidge, the editor, David Eldred, the designer, and Simon Shelmerdine, the production manager for their help in the preparation of this book. Particular thanks are due to militaria consultant Ulric of England, assisted by Andrew Steven of Drew's Militia, for making his outstanding collection of militaria available for photography; to Graham Walser, Kevin Hewitt and Jamie Govier of A C Cooper Neg and Print; and to David Morrison for photographing the author's collection.

We are also grateful to the following individuals and institutions for permission to use the photographs on the pages noted below.

Archiv Gerstenberg 155 (both)
BPL 8 (both), 10 (top), 12 (top), 13 (top), 14 (top left), 15 (top), 28 (top left), 44 (all 3), 45 (top), 49 (below), 51 (top), 67, 69 (below), 73 (top), 74 (below), 75 (top), 76 (bottom), 77, 81 (top), 86 (bottom pair), 87 (top), 91 (top), 99 (top), 101 (top), 110 (both), 112 (top), 118 (top), 121, 123, 126 (below), 144, 146, 147, 148
Bundesarchiv 9 (both), 10 (below), 11 (both), 13 (below), 14 (bottom right), 20-21, 22 (both), 23, 24 (top), 26 (top), 27 (below), 26 (top right &

bottom pair), 38 (below), 50, 53, 54, 56, 60, 64-5, 68 (below), 69 (top), 81 (below bottom left), 90, 92 (bottom pair), 114 (below), 116 (both), 129 (below), 139 (below), 145, 156
Robert Hunt Picture Library 149 (below), 151 (top), 153 (below)
Imperial War Museum 12 (below), 24 (below), 51 (below), 66 (top), 70 (below), 72 (both), 73 (below), 74 (top), 75 (below), 76 (top pair), 78, 79 (below), 81 (bottom right), 82 (top), 92 (top), 99 (below), 101 (below), 107, 113, 114 (top), 118 (below), 119, 125, 126 (top), 135, 142-3, 149 (top)
Robin Lumsden Collection 16, 17 (top), 25, 25 (below), 27 (top), 31, 33 (both), 39 (right), 42 (top), 58 (top), 79 (top), 84 (bottom pair), 88 (top),

93, 141 (both), 152 (top)
Ulric of England (P O Box 285, Epsom, Surrey, KT17 2YJ) 14 (bottom left), 15 (below), 17 (below), 18, 19, 29, 30 (all 3), 32, 36 (both), 37, 38 (top), 39 (top), 40, 41, 42 (below), 43, 45 (below), 46, 47, 48 (both), 49 (top pair), 52, 55 (both), 58 (below), 57, 59, 61, 66 (below), 68 (top), 70 (top), 71, 80, 82 (below), 83, 84 (top), 85, 86 (top), 87 (below), 88 (below), 89, 91 (below), 94 (both), 95, 96, 97, 98, 100, 102, 103, 104, 105, 106 (both), 108, 109, 111 (both), 117, 120, 122, 127, 129 (top), 130, 131, 132, 133, 136, 137, 138, 139 (top), 140, 151 (below), 152 (below), 157 (all 3)